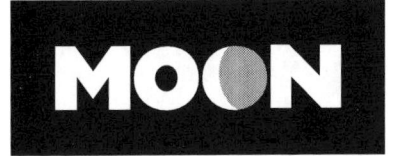

MOON SPOTLIGHT

VIRGINIA'S SHENANDOAH

KATIE GITHENS

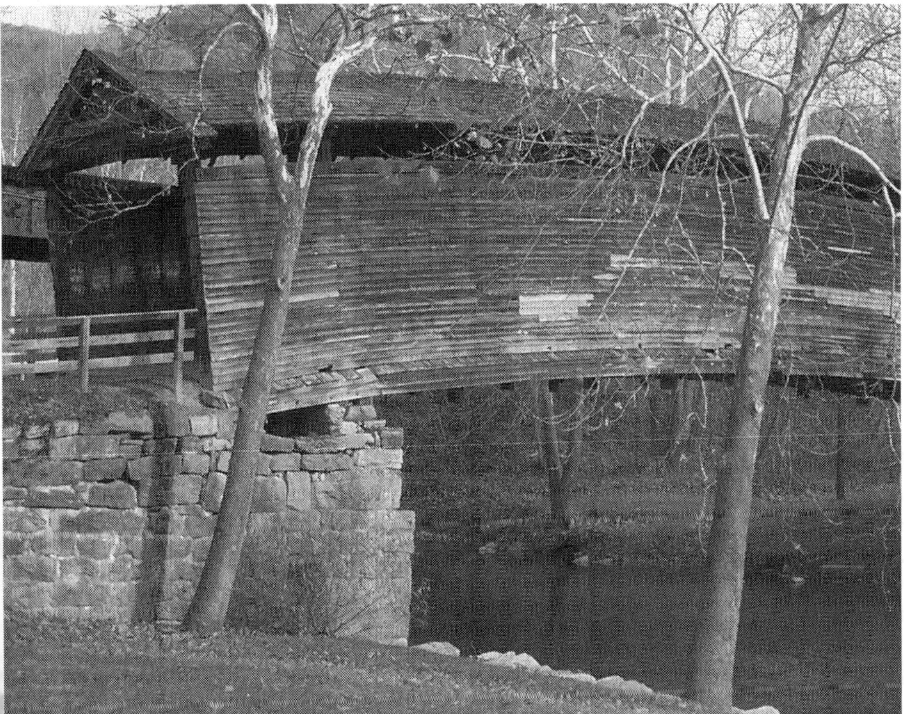

Contents

The Shenandoah 7
Planning Your Time 8
- Access 9
- Resources 12

Winchester and Vicinity 12
History 12
Sights 13
U-Pick Orchards 14
Entertainment 15
Shopping 15
Events 15
Accommodations 15
Food 16
Information 17
Near Winchester 17
- Berryville 17
- White Post 17
- Middletown 18
- Cedar Creek Battlefield and Belle Grove Plantation 18

The Northern Valley 19
Front Royal 19
- Sights 19
- Recreation 20
- Shopping 20
- Events 20
- Accommodations and Camping 20
- Food 21
- Information 21
- Near Front Royal 21
Strasburg 22

West of the Interstate 22
- Bryce Resort 22
- Orkney Springs 22
- Mount Jackson 22

New Market and Vicinity 22
- New Market Battlefield State Historical Park 23
- Commercial Caves 23
- Other Activities 23
- Shopping 24
- Accommodations 24
- Food 24
- Information 24

Luray 24
- ◖ Luray Caverns 24
- Other Diversions and Recreation 26
- Events 26
- Accommodations 26
- Camping 27
- Food 27
- Information 27
- Sperryville 27

Shenandoah National Park .. 28
History 29
Habitats 29
- Flora 30
- Fauna 31
Access 31
- Fees 31
- When to Go 32
◖ Hiking 32
- Easy Hikes 32
- Moderate Hikes 33
- Strenuous Hikes 34

Accommodations,
  Camping, and Services 34
Information 35
  Maps and Information 35
  Visitors Centers and
    Entrance Stations 36

Harrisonburg and Vicinity ... 36
History 36
Sights 37
  Court Square 37
  Virginia Quilt Museum 37
  James Madison University 37
Entertainment 38
Shopping 38
Events 38
Accommodations 39
Food 39
Information 40
Near Harrisonburg 40
  Farmers Markets 40
  Dayton 40
  Green Valley Book Fair 40
  Massanutten Resort 41
  Natural Chimneys Regional Park ... 41
  ◖ Grand Caverns Regional Park ... 41

Staunton and Vicinity 42
History 42
Sights 43
  ◖ Frontier Culture Museum 44
  Woodrow Wilson
    Presidential Library & Museum ... 45
  Other Landmarks 45
Entertainment and
  Recreation 45

Shopping 46
Events 46
Accommodations 47
Food 48
Information 49
Getting There and Around 49
Near Staunton 49
  ◖ Polyface Farms 49
Waynesboro 50

Allegheny Highlands 50
Outdoor Recreation 50
Access 51
Monterey 51
  Recreation 51
  Shopping 51
  Events 51
  Accommodations 51
  Food 52
  Information 52
  Near Monterey 52
Warm Springs 53
  Recreation 53
  Accommodations and Food 53
On the Road to Hot Springs 54
Hot Springs 54
  ◖ The Homestead 54
Douthat State Park 55

Lexington 55
Sights 55
  Washington and Lee University 55
  Virginia Military Institute 56
  Stonewall Jackson House 57

    Stonewall Jackson Cemetery 57
    Boxerwood Gardens 59
    Museum of Military Memorabilia 59
    Virginia Horse Center 59

Entertainment and Recreation . . . 59
    Theaters 59
    Nightlife 60
    Tours 60
    Outdoor Recreation 60

Shopping 61

Events 61

Accommodations 62

Food 62

Information 63

South of Lexington 64
◖ **Natural Bridge** 64
    History 64
    The Bridge 64
    Other Sights 65
    Accommodations and Food 65
    Near Natural Bridge 66

Blue Ridge Parkway 66
    Access 67
    Flora and Fauna 67
    Camping 67
    Rockfish Gap to Sherando Lake 67
    Sherando Lake to Otter Creek 68
    Otter Creek to Roanoke 68
    Information 68

VIRGINIA'S SHENANDOAH

© ALEX GUERRERO

THE SHENANDOAH

"To everyone, especially to those who live in narrow streets where automobiles are thicker than ants in an ant hill and where trolleys clang, sirens screech, and people rush about, we say, come to this beautiful Blue Ridge area for recreation . . ." So began one letter, written in the 1920s, encouraging the creation of Shenandoah National Park. Today, Shenandoah entices visitors for much the same reasons.

But what *is* the Shenandoah, exactly? The word comes from a Native American term meaning "beautiful daughter of the stars," which should give you a clue as to this corner of Virginia's deep and glittering legacy.

In name, it's a lazy-rolling river—two, actually, born in the valleys on the west side of the Blue Ridge. The North and South Forks of the Shenandoah River flow northeast before joining near Front Royal and entering West Virginia. By the time it reaches the Potomac near Harpers Ferry, the Shenandoah has become the larger river's main tributary. It's the perfect waterway for fishing, tubing, or canoeing: slow, winding, and lined with green most of the way.

In legend, the Shenandoah refers to the wide, fertile valley dividing the Blue Ridge Mountains from the Alleghenies—which was elevated to near-mythic status by some of the most dramatic fighting of the Civil War. The fruitful soil drew settlers centuries ago, as first- or second-generation German farmers moved down from Pennsylvania to the valley where, it was said, the summer grass grew high enough to tie across a horse's saddle.

© KATIE GITHENS

HIGHLIGHTS

◖ **Luray Caverns:** The Shenandoah has most of the state's commercial caverns, including this, the largest and most spectacular on the East Coast (page 24).

◖ **Hiking in Shenandoah National Park:** Waterfalls, windswept ridgetops, and the Appalachian Trail, steps away from Skyline Drive, are just some of the attractions you'll see hoofing it through Virginia's premier outdoor destination (page 32).

◖ **Grand Caverns Regional Park:** Cathedral Hall is the highlight of this, another astounding network of caves. Be sure to check out the Civil War-era "graffiti" (page 41).

◖ **Frontier Culture Museum:** Learn what rural life was like in the 18th and 19th centuries at Staunton's first-rate Frontier Culture Museum. The buildings, farming techniques, and even the livestock are all rigorously authentic (page 44).

◖ **Polyface Farms:** Hop on a hay bale for a tour of one of the most sustainable farms in the nation (page 49).

◖ **The Homestead:** Depending on the season, you can golf, ski, or just relax with a soothing soak at the most venerable and lavish resort hotel in the state (page 54).

◖ **Natural Bridge:** Despite all the commercial hoopla surrounding it, it's still an impressive – and beautiful – stretch of stone. Bonus points for spotting George Washington's initials carved into the base (page 64).

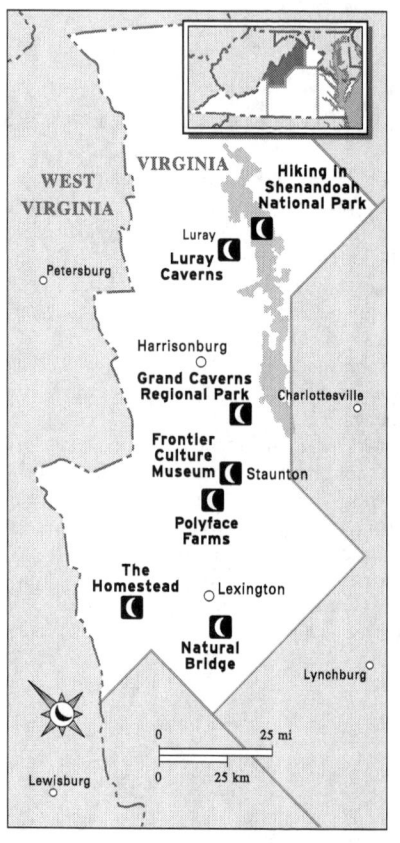

LOOK FOR ◖ TO FIND RECOMMENDED SIGHTS, ACTIVITIES, DINING, AND LODGING.

During the war the valley's productivity and strategic importance almost proved to be her undoing. Over three years, the area endured more battles than any other region in the country, and in so doing, buried tragedy and lore beneath the rich farmland.

In essence, the Shenandoah is equal parts legend and locale, embodied in the rich odors of farmland in morning mist, snow on ragged granite peaks, and the simple pleasures of small-town hospitality evident even in the larger cities.

PLANNING YOUR TIME

Aside from its intangible enticements of atmosphere, the Shenandoah is replete with things to do and see. Set aside at least 4–5 days to hit the highlights. The approach is obviously linear, but Winchester and Staunton both make good staging points from the north and south ends of the valley, respectively. Several good half- and full-day excursions are possible from Winchester, including the towns of White Post and Middletown. Moving south down the valley, **Luray Caverns** and **Grand Caverns** are two of the state's best subterranean attractions. Head up, not down, to reach **Shenandoah National Park,** which you can access from the north, south, or middle entrances.

History fans should be sure not to miss the living exhibits at the **Frontier Culture Museum** near Staunton. While near this city, take a farm tour at **Polyface Farms** and find out what on earth an "Eggerator" is. The Allegheny Highlands make a good two- or three-day excursion from Staunton; head up to Monterey and swing by the **Homestead** on your way back for some golf, spa treatments, or skiing in the winter. Lexington and the famous **Natural Bridge** can be combined into another good day trip from Staunton. You could easily take a week driving from Front Royal to the North Carolina border along the crest of the Blue Ridge, following the Skyline Drive through Shenandoah National Park and the Blue Ridge Parkway thereafter.

Access

I-81 runs the length of the valley along the well-worn route of the Old Valley Pike, once worn deep into the soil by native tribes, European settlers, and Civil War troops. As one of the main north–south routes in the mid-Atlantic, this interstate is clogged with 18-wheelers, which use the route as a toll-free alternative to I-95. (The situation is getting so bad there is talk of building a second four-lane "truckway" parallel to the interstate.) The older, more scenic route of the Old Valley Pike lives on as U.S. 11, worlds away from the interstate, although the two are often within sight and sound of each other. Up north, I-66 leads to Front Royal and the mountains for the weekend hordes from Washington, D.C.

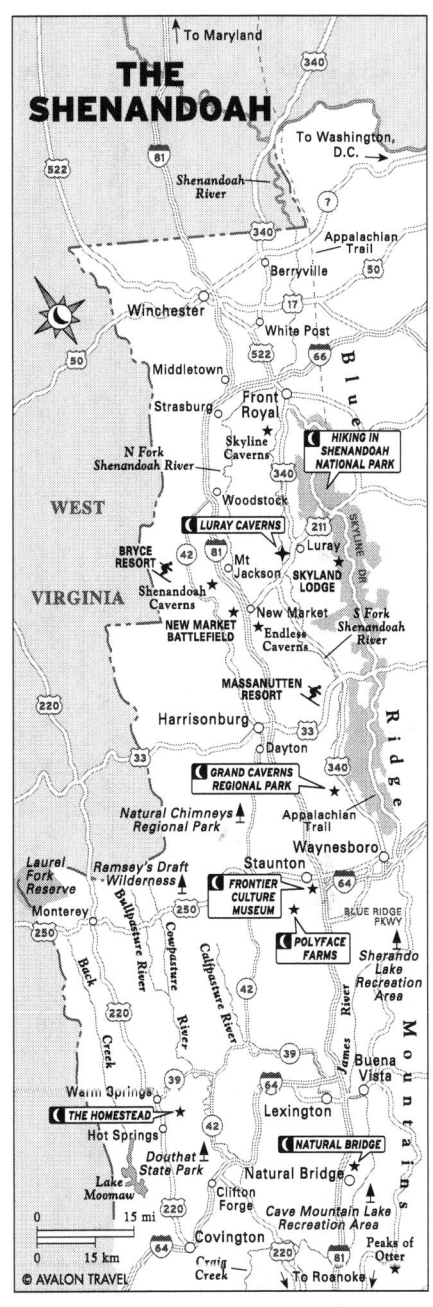

CIVIL WAR IN THE SHENANDOAH

As the Civil War slowly tore through Virginia, the strategic value of the Shenandoah made it crucial to the strategies of both sides. The valley was not only the fertile breadbasket of the Confederacy, but it could also allow troops to march unseen practically to the steps of Washington, D.C. – or, in the other direction, to flank Richmond. "If the valley is lost," declared Stonewall Jackson, "Virginia is lost." The Rebel commander would add his own legend to the two short but bloody years that transformed a pastoral landscape into a smoking wasteland.

SPRING 1862: JACKSON'S VALLEY CAMPAIGN

Robert E. Lee's orders to Jackson were simple: defend the valley, and prevent Federal reinforcements from joining the attack on Richmond. With that in mind, Jackson pitted his 17,000 troops against heavy odds in an incredible display of cunning, endurance, and luck. In seven weeks, Jackson's famous "foot cavalry" – consisting of the 2nd, 4th, 5th, 27th, and 33rd Virginia infantry regiments and the elite Rockbridge Artillery – fought four battles and six skirmishes, marched more than 600 miles, and eventually immobilized and inflicted casualties (twice as many as they suffered) on some 60,000 Federals.

"There are two things never to be lost sight of by a military commander," said Jackson. "Always mystify, mislead, and surprise the enemy if possible...[and] never fight against heavy odds, if by possible maneuvering you can hurl your own force on only a part, and the weakest part, of your enemy and crush it." Not surprisingly, he employed a strategy of surprise and deception that suited the uneven terrain perfectly and had his dogged troops showing up whenever and wherever they were least expected. Jackson realized that speed was of the essence, and once led his troops 350 miles in

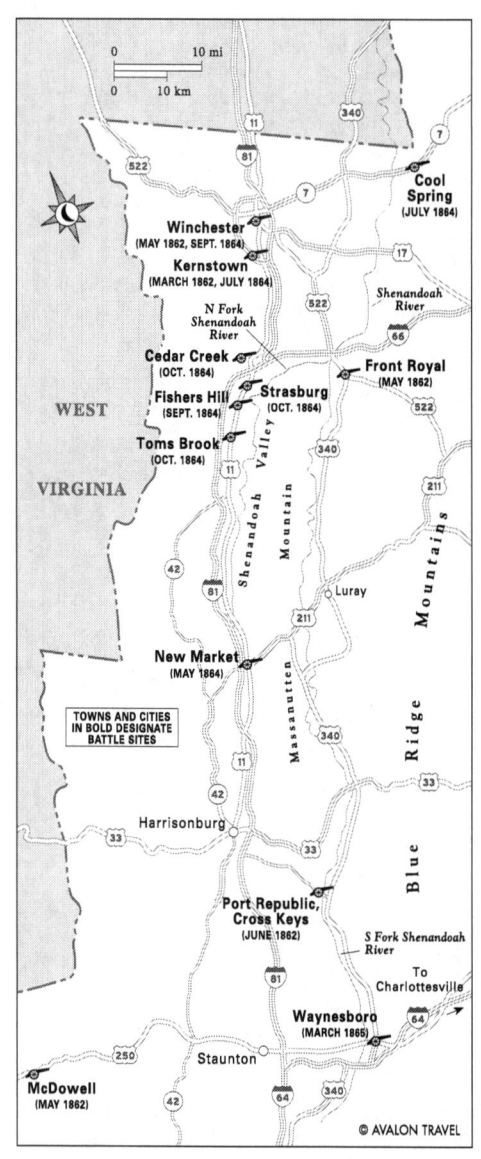

30 days. His tactics worked: As of 1864, the Stonewall Brigade had yet to be driven from a field that it defended.

At the First Battle of Kernstown, on March 23, 1862, Jackson attacked a force he thought to be only a few regiments strong, but which turned out to be Gen. James Shields' entire division. Both sides raced for the cover of a wall in the middle of an open field. The Confederates won, though they eventually had to retreat in the face of overwhelming numbers. The Rebels did, however, manage to keep Shields from joining McClellan's peninsular campaign.

On May 3, Jackson mystified even his own subordinates when he ordered half his army to march eastward out of the valley. Almost to Charlottesville, the troops suddenly found themselves herded onto railroad cars and shipped back to Staunton. There they disembarked and marched off for a surprise attack at McDowell on May 8, forcing Union troops under Gen. Robert Milroy to flee into West Virginia.

With help from the spirited spy Belle Boyd, the Confederates captured Front Royal on May 23 after joining with Jubal Early's command in a surprising move and passing through a gap in Massanutten Mountain. During this battle, members of the 1st Maryland Division from each side found themselves facing, greeting, and then fighting their own neighbors and relatives.

The First Battle of Winchester, on May 25, followed a race toward the important supply city that was lost by Union Maj. Gen. Nathaniel Banks. At sunset, Banks, believing the fighting ended, went upstairs to take a bath. Under Jackson, though, the Confederate attacks continued, sending the Union troops scurrying in retreat toward Washington, D.C. (When Banks asked one retreating soldier if he loved his country, the man replied, "Yes sir, and I'm trying to get back to it as fast as I can.") Pursuit was eventually called off because Jackson's men were too worn out from marching the previous nights.

Two more victories in June near Port Republic secured the Confederate hold on the valley. On June 8, Gen. Richard S. Ewell sent a larger army under Gen. John C. Fremont packing, and the next day Jackson defeated Brig. Gen. Erasmus Tyler.

In a tragic turn of events, Jackson was accidentally killed by his own men following the Confederate triumph at Chancellorsville one year later.

SUMMER 1864: THE TIDE TURNS

As the war dragged on, Lincoln and his Union commanders realized they would have to bring the South to its knees by any means possible to keep the war from continuing indefinitely. Soon after the Battle of New Market on May 15, in which 10 VMI cadets were killed, Union Lt. Gen. Ulysses S. Grant began a massive statewide offensive intended to end the war once and for all. Lee sent Lt. Gen. Jubal Early to defend the valley. Early's Maryland Campaign, as it became known, began with successes at Cool Spring on July 19 and the Second Battle of Kernstown on July 24. By August, Early had his sights set on Washington, D.C., itself.

Embarrassed by the continued defeats and alarmed by the threat to the capital, Grant realized that the Union had to win the valley at all costs. He sent Maj. Gen. Philip Sheridan south with orders to raze the Shenandoah so completely "that a crow flying over it will have to carry his provender [provisions] with him." Sheridan's Valley Campaign spelled doom for the area as surely as Jackson's had meant its temporary salvation. Early's 12,000 remaining troops found themselves facing 40,000 Union soldiers who advanced down the valley slaughtering livestock, ruining fields, and putting buildings to the torch. Scattered stone foundations still recall the frenzy of destruction remembered for generations as "The Burning."

The Battle of Opequon (Third Winchester), on September 19, was the largest in the valley, leaving 5,000 Federal and 3,500 Confederate casualties in its wake. Despite the numbers, it was considered a Union victory. Three more wins – Fishers Hill on September 22, Toms Brook on October 9, and Cedar Creek (near Strasburg) on October 18 – marked the beginning of the end for the Confederate hold on the valley. At the Battle of Waynesboro, on March 2, 1865, Sheridan crushed Early's remaining forces and condemned the South to defeat.

The Blue Ridge is pierced by another interstate (I-64), roughly paralleled by the Amtrak line from Charlottesville to West Virginia via Staunton, and several smaller roads (U.S. 211 from Luray, U.S. 33 from Harrisonburg, and U.S. 60 from Lexington).

Resources

The **Shenandoah Valley Travel Association** (540/740-3132 or 800/847-4878, www.visitshenandoah.org) can provide more information on touring the area. ShenandoahValley.com is another useful website.

Winchester and Vicinity

A map of Virginia is like a salute to our Second Amendment rights, what with city names like Remington and, of course, Winchester. Known for its apple blossoms and Civil War battles, Winchester (pop. 25,000) has alternately enjoyed and endured its position as the gateway to the northern Shenandoah Valley. The largest and fastest-growing city in Virginia's apple heartland of Frederick and Clarke Counties, Winchester is surrounded by acres and acres of orchards, filled with delicate buds in the spring and teams of migrant harvest workers in the fall. From padded shoulder buckets to wooden crates in the backs of rumbling trucks, the fruit eventually makes its way to dozens of processing plants near town that infuse the air with the sweet smell of cider, vinegar, apple butter, and applesauce in the making. More than half of each yearly crop of 200–300 million pounds is sold fresh across the country.

Several natives of this region have gone on to nationwide fame, including progressive 1920s governor Harry Byrd. Country singer Patsy Cline hailed from the nearby town of Gore and worked in Gaunt's Drug Store at the corner of South Loudoun Street and Valley Avenue. She is buried in the Shenandoah Memorial Park cemetery, and a boulevard was named in her honor east of the interstate.

The quaint Old Town Pedestrian Mall (www.oldtownwinchesterva.com), on Loudoun Street between Piccadilly and Cork, is crowded with restaurants.

History

Virginia's oldest city west of the Blue Ridge, Winchester began as a Shawnee campground that was settled by Pennsylvania Quakers in 1732. Settlers soon arrived from all over Europe, including Scotch-Irish, Welsh, English, and French. Germans left their mark in trim houses set flush against sidewalks with tidy gardens in back.

In 1748, an eager red-haired 16-year-old

PATSY CLINE CHRONOLOGY

1932	Born Virginia Patterson Hensley in Winchester
1957	Records "Walkin' After Midnight," which hit #2 on country charts and #12 on pop charts
1958	Moves to Nashville, joins Grand Ole Opry
1961-1962	#1 Female Recording Artist; records Willie Nelson's "Crazy"
1962	#1 country song "I Fall to Pieces"
1963	Dies at age 30 in a plane crash in Tennessee
1973	Inducted into Country Music Hall of Fame
1992	Commemorative stamp issued
1994	Inducted into Cowgirl Hall of Fame
1995	*Greatest Hits* album sells six million copies
	Honored with Grammy Lifetime Achievement Award

arrived to survey thousands of rolling acres belonging to Lord Fairfax. Within a decade, George Washington had set about building Fort Loudoun to protect the frontier town from Indian attacks and French encroachment. Soon he was elected to his first political office in the House of Burgesses.

During the Civil War, Winchester saw as much action as any city in Virginia. On the cusp of the Shenandoah Valley, with Maryland less than 50 miles to the north, Winchester changed hands 72 times during the course of the war—13 times in one day. Some of these capitulations were questionable—a single soldier left in town after the opposition retreated, for instance—but no fewer than five major battles were fought within the city limits. The Third Battle of Winchester (aka Opequon), on September 19, 1864, was the largest fought in the valley. Confederate forces under Lt. Gen. Jubal Early killed more than 5,000 of Sheridan's Federal troops, but the battle was still considered a Union victory. Thousands of wounded were brought here from Gettysburg and Antietam, helping fill close to 8,000 graves in two major cemeteries along Woodstock Lane—Stonewall for the Confederates, National for the Federals.

SIGHTS

The **Museum of the Shenandoah Valley** (901 Amherst St., 540/662-1473 or 888/556-5799, www.shenandoahmuseum.org, 10 A.M.–4 P.M. Tues.–Sun., house and gardens Mar.–Nov. only) combines the 18th-century homestead of Winchester founder James Wood, six acres of

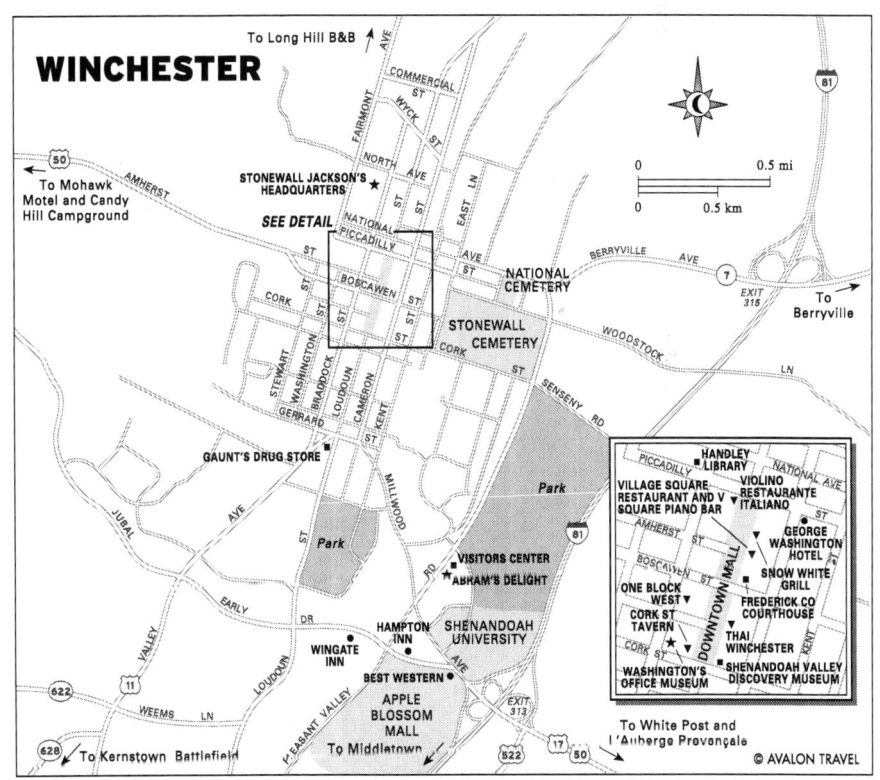

spectacular gardens, including an arched tunnel of flowering crab apple trees, and a modern museum for an in-depth overview of the valley's history, art, and culture. Opened in 2005, the museum displays fine art, antiques, and a beguiling gallery of miniature rooms and houses. Admission to all is $12 adults, $10 children 7–18, with less expensive options to visit the house, gardens, or museum only.

Block tickets to Winchester's three main historical sights can be purchased ($10 adults, $4 children 7–18) at any of the three locations. Separate admission is also available ($5/$2.50). Abram's Delight, Stonewall Jackson's Headquarters, and George Washington's Office Museum are all open 10 A.M.–4 P.M. Monday–Saturday, noon–4 P.M. Sunday April–October.

Abram's Delight (1340 S. Pleasant Valley Rd., 540/662-6519, www.winchesterhistory.org), the oldest home in Winchester, sits across from the visitors center and next to pleasant Wilkins Lake Park. This stone building was built by Isaac Hollingsworth in 1754 to replace a log cabin built by his father, Abraham, who had called his 582 acres "a delight to behold." The limestone main house served as the city's first Quaker meetinghouse. Five generations of Hollingsworths furnished the home with what are now beautiful antiques, and rope beds upstairs had to be tightened every night with a special crank (hence the phrase "sleep tight"). Abraham's ghost is said to move things around when nobody's looking.

The 1854 Gothic Revival building that served as **Stonewall Jackson's Headquarters** (415 N. Braddock St., 540/667-3242, www.winchesterhistory.org) originally belonged to Lt. Col. Lewis Moore, great-grandfather of Mary Tyler Moore (who donated the reproduction gilt wallpaper). The building was taken over by the Confederate general from late 1861 to the start of his Valley Campaign in 1862. Civil War–era furniture and relics include original Confederate flags, uniforms, and Jackson's prayer book and camp table. Heft an 1861 Springfield rifle and try to figure out whether *you* could have handled the percussion caps, minnie ball bullets, and ramrod quickly enough to load and fire it three times in one minute.

Between September 1755 and December 1756, future founding father George Washington, still a 23-year-old colonel in the Virginia militia, organized the frontier town's Revolutionary War defenses from a three-room structure preserved today as **George Washington's Office Museum** (32 W. Cork St., 540/662-4412, www.winchesterhistory.org). The museum is filled with Revolutionary War memorabilia, antique surveying tools, and an interactive map of early Winchester. Bloodstains under one window bear witness to one of the city's many battles, and there is a lock of Washington's hair on display.

The **Old Court House Civil War Museum** in the Frederick County Courthouse (20 N. Loudoun St., 540/542-1145, www.civilwarmuseum.org, 10 A.M.–5 P.M. Wed.–Sat., 1–5 P.M. Sun., $5 adults, $3 children 5–17) contains excavated relics from the war that illustrate the lives of common soldiers. The building served as a hospital and prison for both sides. Graffiti left by prisoners on the upstairs walls, including a curse to Confederate president Jefferson Davis by a Union soldier, have been framed behind glass.

At the corner of Braddock and Piccadilly sits the **World's Largest Apple,** built to top a 5,200-pound monument in rival apple town Cornelia, Georgia (which was actually a 1927 gift from Winchester). A few blocks over on the downtown mall, children can try their hand at a mock apple-packing center, one of the many interactive exhibits at the **Shenandoah Valley Discovery Museum** (54 S. Loudoun St., 540/722-2020, www.discoverymuseum.net, 9 A.M.–5 P.M. Mon.–Sat., 1–5 P.M. Sun., $6). You can browse the museum shop for free.

With its extensively carved exterior and three-story rotunda topped by a copper dome, the 1913 **Handley Library** (100 W. Piccadilly St. at Boscawen, 540/662-9041, www.hrl.lib.state.va.us) is considered the best example of beaux arts architecture in the state.

U-PICK ORCHARDS

You can't come to Winchester and not pick a few apples for the ride home. There are at least a half-dozen u-pick orchards within a short drive of town. **Marker-Miller Orchards** (3035 Cedar Creek Grade, 540/662-1980, www.markermillerorchards.com) has 325 acres of familiar varieties like Gala and Granny Smith as well as lesser-known Nittanys and Staymans. The apple-cider donuts at the bakery are the real reason you want to come. **Richards Fruit Market** (6410 Middle Rd., 540/869-1455, www.richardsfruitmarket.com) holds an Apple Festival in October with pony rides, live music, and ice cream to go with slices of apple pie. Apple-picking season usually begins in late August and continues through late November. The Virginia State Apple Board (434/984-0573, www.virginiaapples.org) and the Winchester–Frederick County Visitors Center will have more suggestions.

ENTERTAINMENT

From mid-June to early August, you can enjoy a Broadway performance by the **Shenandoah Summer Music Theatre** (877/580-8025, www.shenandoahsummermusictheatre.com). Tickets for productions such as *Annie, Fiddler on the Roof,* and *Oklahoma!* are around $28. It's based out of Shenandoah University near Abram's Delight.

Look for live music at **Brewbaker's Restaurant** (168 N. Loudoun St., 540/535-0111) and **Sweet Caroline's** (29 W. Cork St., 540/723-8805, www.sweetcarolines.net).

SHOPPING

At the north end of the mall, the **HandWorks Gallery** (150 N. Loudoun St., 540/662-3927) sells unusual and beautiful handicrafts from all over the world, including handcrafted wooden boxes from Poland, batik masks from Indonesia, and Peruvian carved gourds. The **Winchester Book Gallery** (185 N. Loudoun St., 540/667-3444) stocks a large selection of gardening and Civil War titles, as well as cookbooks and children's picture books.

The wood floor and handhewn beams of an old apple-packing warehouse lend the perfect setting for antiques shopping at **Millwood Crossing** (381 Millwood Ave., 540/662-5157), with about 10,000 square feet of antiques and specialty shops.

EVENTS

To usher in spring and its acres of blooming orchards, normally conservative Winchester erupts with pink and green clothing, parades, music, and parties. The first **Shenandoah Apple Blossom Festival** (540/662-3863, www.thebloom.com) was organized in 1924, and except for a break during World War II, it's been going strong ever since. Six days of entertainment, food, and fun, including a circus, a 10K race, and the coronation of the Apple Blossom Queen, take place every May the weekend before Mother's Day.

The **Winchester City Market** is held at the south end of the mall 9 A.M.–1 P.M. on Saturdays during growing season (roughly May–Oct.). Finally, Winchester's **Hot Air Balloon Festival** takes place in mid-October at Historic Long Branch, an 1811 Greek Revival mansion in Millwood. Rides, launches, music, artisans, and wine tasting are all part of the fun. To get there, take Route 624 (Red Gate Rd.) 10 miles east of White Post.

ACCOMMODATIONS

Here is what you'll find in town, but some of the most interesting lodgings in the area are outside the city, in Berryville, White Post, and Middletown.

$50-100

Exit 313 onto U.S. 50 off I-81 has most of Winchester's midpriced hotels, including the **Hampton Inn** (1655 Apple Blossom Dr., 540/667-8011, $80–100) and the **Best Western Lee-Jackson** (711 Millwood Ave., 540/662-4154, $70–80). The **Mohawk Motel** (2754 Northwestern Pike, 540/667-1410, $56) has offered budget quarters for close to 50 years. It's worth the drive out of town (three miles south on Rte. 37 from I-81 exit 317, then two miles west on U.S. 50) for the views.

Four miles from Old Town, the **Long Hill Bed & Breakfast** (547 Apple Pie Ridge Rd., 540/450-0341 or 866/450-0341, www.longhillbb.com) has three rooms for $95. The house is an interesting custom design with stained glass and artwork. Owners George and Rhoda Kriz offer sunny hospitality and award-winning breakfasts. There's a pool table and a vintage pinball machine in the game room downstairs. The gardens outside are certified wildlife habitat, with bird feeders galore. To get there, take Fairmont Avenue north from downtown. It turns into Frederick Pike (Rte. 522) and crosses the Route 37 bypass. Take an immediate right onto Apple Pie Ridge Road, and the turn-off will be on your left.

$100-150

Winchester's **Wingate Inn** (150 Wingate Dr., 540/678-4283, $89) is among the most modern in town, with a business center, conference center, and heated pool. In addition to 145 rooms, the **Travelodge of Winchester** (160 Front Royal Pike, 540/665-0685, $65) has a heated pool and wireless Internet.

$150-250

The **George Washington Hotel** (103 E. Piccadilly St., 540/678-4700, www.wyndham.com/hotels/DCAGW, $120–130) features a Roman bath–style indoor swimming pool and the Dancing Goat restaurant, and is the most opulent place to stay in town. Built in 1924, Winchester's landmark historic hotel features luxurious guest rooms, fireplaces, whirlpool tubs, restaurants, lobby bar, and high-speed Internet.

Camping

Sites at the **Candy Hill Campground** (165 Ward Ave., 540/662-8010 or 800/462-0545, www.candyhill.com) are $35–50. It's open year-round, just beyond the Route 37 bypass, and has a pool, bathhouse, game room, and grocery store.

FOOD
Casual

The snugly casual **Cork Street Tavern** (8 W. Cork St., 540/667-3777, lunch and dinner daily) serves burgers ($7–8), award-winning ribs, and other hearty entrées ($12–23) in front of a big stone fireplace and bar. The building has quite a history; some parts date to the 1830s, it was shelled during the Civil War (it's said ghosts still haunt the place), and as the Rustic Tavern it survived the Depression and World War II.

On the downtown mall, the **Snow White Grill** (159 N. Loudoun St., 540/662-5955, lunch Mon.–Sat., open late Fri.–Sat.) is a diner that's usually crammed with locals who come in for ice cream and cheap eats ($2–6), especially the mini-burgers with grilled onions and pickles on a steamed roll. The grill has been serving inexpensive lunch-counter fare since 1949. If you're craving spice, look no further than **Thai Winchester** (24 S. Loudoun St., 540/678-0055, lunch and dinner daily, $8–14).

Upscale

Starting at the north end of the mall, the ◖ **Violino Restaurante Italiano** (181 N. Loudoun St., 540/667-8006, lunch and dinner Mon.–Sat.) serves creative Italian fare that earned four stars in one local review. Franco and Marcella Stocco from Turin offer classic Northern cuisine, graced by excellent sauces, in the $15–35 range, including many vegetarian plates. Reservations recommended.

A bit farther down is the **Village Square Restaurant** (103 N. Loudoun St., 540/667-8961, lunch and dinner Mon.–Sat., brunch Sun.), serving American fare with staid European influences—starting with hand-prepared stock for sauces. There's outdoor seating under a canopy of trees along the mall. Lunch ($8–12) and dinner entrées ($17–29) such as pan-seared rockfish, are excellent. The Sunday champagne brunch ($28) features live music, and the stylish V Square Piano Bar is open until 1 A.M.

Just one block off the mall is, fittingly, ◖ **One Block West** (25 S. Indian Alley, 540/662-1455, lunch and dinner Tues.–Sat.), offering a changing menu of fresh local products, many from Virginia. Lunch plates are mostly $8–14, and dinner entrées ($19–33) such as grilled Virginia lamb loin chop with pesto always have a helpful suggested wine pairing on the menu. As a prelude to dinner, or to find recipes after a delicious meal, check out chef Ed Matthews's blog (http://oneblockwest.blogspot.com).

INFORMATION

The **Winchester-Frederick County Convention and Visitors Bureau** (1400 S. Pleasant Valley Rd., 540/542-1326 or 888/316-6189, www.visitwinchesterva.com, 9 A.M.–5 P.M. daily) has videos of the area, the Civil War, and Patsy Cline, a small shrine to the singer, and brochures of walking and driving tours.

NEAR WINCHESTER
Berryville

For a change of pace from the usual hotels, motels, and bed-and-breakfasts, consider a spiritual stay at the **Holy Cross Abbey** (901 Cool Spring Ln., 540/955-4383, www.hcava.org), one of 17 working Trappist monasteries in the country. Members of the Cistercian Order of the Strict Observance, begun in France in 1098, live a quiet life on 1,200 acres in the rolling Blue Ridge foothills alongside the Shenandoah River. The monastery's main means of support is a bakery, where the monks find time, between their six daily services, to turn out 24,000 famous fruitcakes a year.

An elegant guesthouse located a short distance from the monastery can be rented by anyone interested in joining the monks in quietness and prayer. Retreats run Monday–Friday for a suggested donation of $300–500 per person ($75 deposit) for the duration of the stay, including meals, or Friday–Sunday ($150–300 pp, $75 deposit). Guests are welcome to join in the services, sung liturgy, and family-style meals. Reservations should be made as far in advance as possible. A gift shop and information center (1:15–5 P.M. Sun.–Fri., 10 A.M.–noon and 1:15–5 P.M. Sat., longer hours mid-Oct.–Dec.) sells Cistercian publications and monastery products, including Trappist preserves, creamed honey, fudge, and bread, but not, alas, any abbey ales.

To get there, follow Route 7 east to Berryville, turning left immediately before crossing the Shenandoah River onto Route 603, and watch for a sign on the right after one mile.

White Post

Eight miles south of Winchester at the intersection of U.S. 522, U.S. 340, and Route 277 looms **Dinosaur Land** (3848 Stonewall Jackson Hwy., 540/869-2222, www.dinosaurland.com, 9:30 A.M.–5:30 or 6:30 P.M. daily Mar.–Dec., $5 adults, $4 children 2–10), a Jurassic-themed landmark that's been around for decades. More than 50 dinosaur replicas, including all those tongue-tying names your kids know by heart—brontosaurus, stegosaurus, yaleosaurus, and saltoposuchus—stand next to a 60-foot shark, a 70-foot octopus, and a 20-foot cobra (and don't miss the fake caveman).

In the same town but at the other end of the cultural spectrum is (**L'Auberge Provençale** (13630 Lord Fairfax Hwy., 540/837-1375 or 800/638-1702, www.laubergeprovencale.com). Innkeepers Alain and Celeste Borel have created a small, charming French country inn in the middle of the fields and pastures of the Shenandoah. Three buildings huddle near an expansive flower garden, full of tulips in the spring and sunflowers every fall. Over the years the American Historic Inns, the *Washington Post,* AOL, and *Washingtonian* magazine have all called it one of the most romantic inns in the country. Alain, the French-born chef, draws regular visitors from the nation's capital for a taste of his native Avignon in the dining rooms of the 18th-century stone manor house. Fresh ingredients from the gardens and local farmers add the final touch to gourmet candlelit dinners featuring foie gras, smoked rabbit, and fresh Shenandoah trout—and that's just for appetizers. Breakfast is almost as much of a production: Scones, salmon, poached eggs, and croissants may all grace your plate. The four-diamond restaurant is open to visitors as well as guests for dinner Wednesday–Monday, with a three-course ($58 pp) or five course ($88 pp) meal, or a seven-course chef's tasting menu ($115) including dessert. It also offers a Sunday bistro lunch.

Provençal fabrics, canopy beds, and fireplaces fill seven guest rooms and four suites available for $165–325. Two more suites and another room ($245–295) are available in the Villa La Campagnette, set on 18 wooded acres three miles from L'Auberge. This equally impressive spread, decorated like a Mediterranean villa, has a brick terrace next to a pool and outdoor whirlpool tub.

Middletown

Antiques stores and a curious mix of old and new houses line U.S. 11, called Main Street as it passes through the center of Middletown. There you'll find the **Wayside Inn** (7783 Main St., 540/869-1797 or 877/869-1797, www.alongthewayside.com), one of the oldest inns in the United States. It received its first guests in 1797 as Wilkerson's Tavern, and it later served as a stagecoach rest stop and way station for soldiers from both sides of the Civil War. With the arrival of the automobile, it became America's first motor inn, regaining much of its antique charm during a restoration in the 1960s.

An antique parlor off a lobby welcomes guests with chiming clocks and brick-and-stone fireplaces. Antiques and books are everywhere, including a combination chess and cribbage board. The stately Colonial dining room of Larrick's Tavern dates to the 1720s, with lunch entrées for $8–11. Traditional dinner plates such as peanut soup at the Wayside Restaurant run $15–25. Each of the 22 rooms has a distinct personality, and the hotel offers popular romantic escapes for honeymoons and anniversaries that include champagne, breakfast in bed, and a special late checkout. Rooms are $100–170.

Just south of the inn, the small, intimate **Wayside Theater** (7853 Main St., 540/869-1776, www.waysidetheater.org) began as a movie house in the 1940s before being converted with a stage in 1962. The second-oldest professional theater in Virginia, it's now under the management of a nonprofit community foundation, which has welcomed actors such as Susan Sarandon and Kathy Bates. Tickets are $23–30 adults, $10 children under 17.

Cedar Creek Battlefield and Belle Grove Plantation

In the predawn mist of October 19, 1864, 17,000 famished Confederates under Lt. Gen. Jubal Early made a surprise attack on 30,000 Union troops. The Rebels soon had the larger force on the run to the north of Middletown ("they jumped up running," recalled one attacker), but Maj. Gen. Philip Sheridan managed to gallop from Winchester in time to rally his forces, a ride later celebrated in song and legend. More than three times as many Confederate soldiers were killed or wounded as Union soldiers as the Federals pushed their opponents back to the south and eventually out of the valley altogether, signaling the end of Confederate military power in the Shenandoah.

In 2002, Congress approved the creation of the **Cedar Creek and Bell Grove National Historical Park** (www.nps.gov/cebe), encompassing the battlefield and the historic Belle Grove mansion nearby. It's intended to be a different sort of Park Service unit; private landowners and organizations will still be able to live, work, and operate within the park's 3,000 acres. As of 2010, though, the National Park Service hadn't yet put any visitor facilities in place.

In the meantime, head to the Cedar Creek Battlefield **visitors center** (540/869-2064 or 888/628-1864, www.cedarcreekbattlefield.org, 10 A.M.–4 P.M. Mon.–Sat., 1–4 P.M. Sun., Apr.–Oct.), run by a nonprofit foundation on Route 11 one mile south of Middletown. The fields have changed little in the years since the battle, which is reenacted with gusto every year on the weekend closest to October 19. More than 5,000 participants take part under the gaze of 20,000 spectators, usually just as the fall leaves are reaching their colorful peak.

Belle Grove Plantation (540/869-2028, www.bellegrove.org, 10 A.M.–4 P.M. Mon.–Sat., 1–5 P.M. Sun., Apr.–Oct., $8 adults, $4 children 6–12) sits in the middle of the battlefield opposite the visitors center. Once one of the valley's most prestigious homes, it was built in 1794–1797 by Major Isaac Hite Jr. with design help from Thomas Jefferson. Sheridan used the mansion as his headquarters for his devastating march down the valley, and James and Dolley Madison later honeymooned here. A quilt and fabric shop fills the basement, and Colonial craft demonstrations are held in the smokehouse, icehouse, and blacksmith shops.

The Northern Valley

FRONT ROYAL

Known as Hell Town during its frontier days, this riverside city is thought to have been unintentionally renamed by an exasperated Colonial drill sergeant. His repeated orders for his troops to "Front the royal oak!" in the center of town (oaks were considered the royal tree of England) struck someone's fancy, and the name stuck. In the Civil War, Stonewall Jackson captured Front Royal in May 1862 with the help of spy Belle Boyd.

Today, a long bridge over the Shenandoah River leads to tree-lined Royal Avenue (U.S. 340). Turn left onto East Main Street at the Warren County Courthouse to reach the Village Commons with its gazebo, big red caboose, and the town visitors center. Front Royal serves as the northern gateway to Shenandoah National Park and the Blue Ridge, which rises to the south of town.

Sights

Learn more about life during the days of Belle Boyd, along with details about her spy life, at the **Belle Boyd Cottage** (101 Chester St., 540/636-1446, www.warrenheritagesociety.org, 10 A.M.–4 P.M. Mon.–Fri., 11 A.M.–4 P.M. Sat.–Sun. June–Oct., $3).

MATA HARI OF THE CONFEDERACY

Belle Boyd, the Confederacy's most colorful secret agent, was born in Martinsburg, Virginia, in 1843 and reveled in attention from an early age. With the arrival of the Civil War, the vivacious young woman used her quick mind and feminine charms to coax military secrets from Union troops and pass them on to Confederate officers. By age 21, she had achieved a measure of infamy within Union forces: She had been reported 30 times, arrested six or seven, and thrown in jail twice. During one stay in Washington, D.C.'s Old Capital Prison, Boyd put intelligence messages in India rubber balls and threw them to an accomplice waiting outside her window.

Fellow Southern belles were shocked at Boyd's life of risk. She often traveled alone, meeting with officers from both sides in their private tents with little concern for decorum. Refusing to disguise her handwriting or encode her messages, the socialite spy found herself an international celebrity called "La Belle Rebelle" in France and "That Secesh Cleopatra" in New York.

Front Royal served as her main base of operations. When a Federal regiment under Gen. Nathaniel P. Banks occupied the city in May 1862, Boyd invited the officers to a ball and plied them for information. After her guests had fallen asleep, she reportedly rode 30 miles in the dead of night to pass the intelligence to Stonewall Jackson, who attacked the next morning and captured three-quarters of the Union forces.

After the war ended, Boyd tried her hand at acting and gave public lectures on her secretive adventures. In 1865, she published *Belle Boyd in Camp and Prison*, a dramatic tell-all of life as a female secret agent. She died in 1900 in Wisconsin.

A local chapter of the United Daughters of the Confederacy owns and operates the **Warren Rifles Confederate Museum** (95 Chester St., 540/636-6982, 9 A.M.–4 P.M. Mon.–Sat., noon–4 P.M. Sun., Apr. 15–Oct., $4), containing a large collection of arms, uniforms, flags, pictures, and personal items that evoke the Civil War exploits of Stonewall Jackson, Mosby's Rangers, J. E. B. Stuart, and Robert E. Lee.

There's an interesting **elephant mural** by nationally known artist Patricia Windrow entitled *The Not-So-National Zoo* on the side of a barn at High and Jackson Streets.

Recreation

Several local outfitters take advantage of the fact that one of Virginia's favorite rafting rivers flows practically through their backyard. Most operate campsites down the South Fork of the Shenandoah for overnight visitors during the floating season of March–November. Prices should include equipment, brief instruction, maps, and shuttle service.

The **Front Royal Canoe Company** (8567 Stonewall Jackson Hwy., 540/635-5440 or 800/270-8808, www.frontroyalcanoe.com) runs canoe, raft, and kayak trips starting at $40, with longer excursions of 2–3 days also available. Tubing ($16 pp) is popular, and it also rents canoes, kayaks, and rafts.

Take a guided horseback ride with **Highlander Horses** (5197 Reliance Rd., 540/636-4523, www.highlanderhorses.com) for $30–90 per person for 1–2 hours. They have year-round access to 200 acres of riding terrain. If you'd like to polish your equine technique, group instruction is $30 per person per hour, and semi-private and private instruction runs $40–50 per person per hour. (Reliance Rd./Rte. 627 is off Rte. 532 north of town.) A flight with **Blue Ridge Hot Air Balloons** (540/622-6325 or 877/743-3247, www.rideair.com) will set you back $200 per person, but the views are wonderful—and the champagne toast afterward doesn't hurt either.

Shopping

On summer weekends and holidays, the **Front Royal Antique and Flea Market** (S. Commerce Ave. btwn. Stonewall Dr. and South St., 540/535-7330) is *the* place for assorted treasures, junk, and crafts spread among 100 booths. The **Royal Oak Bookshop** (207 S. Royal Ave., 540/635-7070) stocks thousands of rare, used, out-of-print, and new books.

Events

Front Royal is home to the **Virginia Wine and Craft Festival** (540/635-3185, www.wineandcraftfestival.com), held the third Saturday of May. In early August, the **Warren County Fair** (540/635-5827, www.warrencountyfair.com) brings a 4-H livestock auction, tractor pull, car show, music, rides, and pageants.

Accommodations and Camping

You can find rooms for $50–65 at the **Budget Inn** (1122 N. Royal Ave., 540/635-2196), for $70–90 at the **Quality Inn Skyline Drive** (10 Commerce Ave., 540/635-3161), and for $55 at the **Twi-Lite Motel** (53 W. 14th St., 540/635-4148), which offers an outdoor pool.

Innkeepers Tom and Kathy Conkey run the impressive Edwardian mansion known as **Killahevlin** (1401 N. Royal Ave., 540/636-7335 or 800/847-6132, www.vairish.com), built by a local limestone baron on one of the highest hilltops in town. A strong Irish influence pervades, from the reproduction wallpaper to the private pub with its oak bar and Irish beer on tap. The four "color" rooms (Green, White, Blue, and Raspberry) are $155–225, while two suites in the early-1900s Tower House out back, near the koi pool and gazebos, cost $255–285.

Lackawanna (236 Riverside Dr., 540/636-7945, www.lackawannabb.com) is a bed-and-breakfast in an 1869 Italianate-style home and a big porch overlooking the junction of the North and South Forks of the Shenandoah River. An outdoor pool is open seasonally, nice for a dip and sunbathing after a long hike in nearby Shenandoah National Park. Accommodations including a filling breakfast are $140–170.

Besides Shenandoah National Park itself, campers should head to Gooney Creek

Campground (7122 Stonewall Jackson Hwy., 540/635-4066, www.gooneycreek.com). Full hookups are $27 and tent sites go for $19. The campground is open April through October.

Food

Cajun-fried catfish and slow-cooked jerk chicken will nourish the body and taste buds at **Soul Mountain Restaurant** (300 E. Main St., 540/636-0070, lunch and dinner Tues.–Sun.) for $13–22. At lunchtime, salads, wraps, and sandwiches come served with pasta salad and fries for $7–11. **Wynn's** (219 E. Main St., 540/635-5956, breakfast and lunch Tues.–Sat.) is a popular breakfast and lunch spot open from 5 A.M. On Saturdays Wynn's serves breakfast all day. **L Dee's Pancake House** (522 E. Main St., 540/635-3791, breakfast and lunch Wed.–Mon.) also offers breakfast all day starting at $3, along with daily lunch specials.

The **Royal Oak Tavern** (101 W. 14th St., 540/551-9953, lunch and dinner daily) serves American standards in a casual setting, including the "best ribs in the Valley." Sandwiches and burgers go for $7–8 (lunch) and entrées run $11–22 (dinner).

Set in the old Proctor Biggs feed mill building next to the town park, the **Main Street Mill** (500 E. Main St., 540/636-3123, lunch and dinner daily) serves sandwiches and burgers for around $5–10 and heartier entrées such as ribs, pork chops, and pastas for $10–16. Dine inside by the animal paintings or out on the patio. There's a tavern upstairs as well.

Above **Element** (206 S. Royal Ave., 540/636-9293, lunch Tues.–Sun., dinner Wed.–Sun.), a casual bistro specializing in gourmet soups, salads, and sandwiches perfect for a picnic, is **Apartment 2G** (540/636-7306, dinner Fri.–Sat.), a snug restaurant with a full bar. Apartment 2G serves five-course dinners on Friday and Saturday ($50) with starters like shrimp with saffron risotto and finishers like roast rack of lamb. The experience is like having dinner in the apartment of a gourmet friend, and everything is prepared on the premises daily. The evening's party trick is that you get to watch the chefs prepare your meal on a closed-circuit camera projected onto TVs in the dining room. As the chefs say, it's an alternative to "the ennui of the countless chain restaurants." Reservations are required.

To satisfy a sweet tooth, go to **Spelunker's Custard** (116 South St., 540/631-0300, lunch and dinner daily) for frozen custard or a chocolate malt. Inexpensive cheeseburgers and Philly cheesesteaks are also on the menu.

Information

The **Front Royal-Warren County Visitor Center** (414 E. Main St., 540/635-5788 or 800/338-2576, www.discoverfrontroyal.com) sits in the restored train station in the town park. Open 9 A.M.–5 P.M. daily.

Near Front Royal

Opened to the public in 1939, **Skyline Caverns** (800/296-4545, www.skylinecaverns.com, 9 A.M.–6 P.M. daily, to 4 P.M. off-season, $16 adults, $8 children 7–13) were discovered a few years earlier by means of a giant sinkhole where the parking lot now sits. The highlights of these caves, otherwise overshadowed by their southern neighbors, are glittering calcite formations called anthodites. These delicate spikes are found in only one other cave in the United States (and there in much smaller quantities). They grow one inch every 7,000 years, and are either pure white or stained brown by iron oxide. Skyline Caverns' crop sprouted in a vacuum left by a receding underground pool.

Throughout the rest of the cave, high, smooth passages evoke the slot canyons of the American southwest. Kids love the Skyline Arrow, an outdoor miniature train that crawls near the entrance. The caverns are on Route 340, about one mile south of Route 55.

One of the newest additions to Virginia's state park system, the **Raymond R. "Andy" Guest Jr. Shenandoah River State Park** (540/622-6840, www.dcr.virginia.gov/state_parks/and.shtml, 8 A.M.–dusk daily, $2–3 per car) encompasses 1,600 rolling acres along the South Fork of the river eight miles south of Front Royal, including 5.6 miles of river frontage. Most people come to fish or boat, but there are also 13 miles of trails and campsites ($20–30).

STRASBURG

One of the earliest settlements in the valley, Strasburg has been a crafts center since being chartered in 1761. A tradition of earthen and stoneware pottery was once manifested in six shops going at once in a section called Pot Town. Antiques are now the main draw of the self-proclaimed "antiques capital of Virginia," with local ceramics running a close second.

Try any of the dozen or so shops in town for furniture, clothing, folk art, and rugs, such as **Vilnis and Company Antiques** (329 N. Massanutten St., 540/465-4405). For a larger-scale approach, stop by the 65,000-square-foot **Strasburg Antique Emporium** (160 N. Massanutten St., 540/465-3711), one of the largest antiques centers in the state. More than 100 dealers and artisans sell vintage clothing, paintings, furniture, jewelry, and more in a former silk mill.

WEST OF THE INTERSTATE
Bryce Resort

Only a few miles from the West Virginia border, this small resort features two chairlifts and eight ski slopes ranging from beginner to expert. Voted the mid-Atlantic's most family-friendly resort in 2008, Bryce Resort is sure to tucker out kids and grown-ups looking for a winter escape. Lift tickets sell for $40 adults and $33 children on weekdays ($57/$50 on weekends), with half-days for $28/$23 ($44/$39). The ski instruction program, developed by German National certified instructor Horst Locher, starts with children as young as four. Night skiing, snowboarding, snow tubing, and ski rentals are all options.

Dine at the Restaurant @ Bryce Resort (540/856-8187, dinner Fri.–Sat., brunch Sun.) or the more informal Copper Kettle Bar & Lounge (lunch and dinner daily, drinks until late). In the summer, an 18-hole, par 71 golf course enjoys mountain views and all the amenities. Guests can also choose from grass skiing (just what the name implies), mountain boarding (ditto), tennis, and boating on Lake Laura.

To get there, take I-81 exit 273 onto Route 263 and head 11 miles to the entrance on the right. For more information on the resort and lodging options, including rental properties, contact the resort directly (540/856-2121 or 800/821-1444, www.bryceresort.com).

Orkney Springs

Five weekends between late May and the end of August are filled with symphony, big band, jazz, and folk music during the **Shenandoah Valley Music Festival** (540/459-3396 or 800/459-3396, www.musicfest.org) in this tiny town in the hills. A benefit ball kicks things off, and ice cream socials and children's concerts are part of the program. Tickets for individual events are $25–40 in the open-air pavilion and $20–27 on the lawn.

The concerts have been held since the early 1960s at the Shrine Mont Retreat and Conference Center, a venerable mineral springs resort dating to the turn of the 20th century. The town is 15 miles west of I-81 exit 273 via Route 263.

Mount Jackson

Originally housed in an old feed store in Middletown when the company began in the 1990s, the **Route 11 Potato Chip Factory** (11 Edwards Way, 540/477-9664 or 800/294-7783, www.rt11.com) was said to be the smallest of its kind in the country. In 2008, the chipmakers expanded into a factory space in Mount Jackson, but everything is still hand-cooked. Watch the spudmasters at work and sample the chips 9 A.M.–5 P.M. Monday–Saturday.

NEW MARKET AND VICINITY

Two major Indian pathways gave this spot on the upper North Fork of the Shenandoah its first official name of Cross Roads. The first inhabitants, the Senedo tribe, were wiped out by the Catawbas from the south when their paths crossed around 1700. In 1796, the town of New Market was established, named after the city in England with a famous racetrack (there was also a racetrack here, to the west of the settlement). A famous Civil War clash nearby left the town with memories of children lost in battle and a three-inch shell hole in a post at the intersection of Breckinridge Lane and Congress Street (U.S. 11 through town).

New Market Battlefield State Historical Park

On May 15, 1864, one of the last Confederate victories in the valley campaign featured a famous charge by Virginia Military Institute (VMI) cadets against a line of Union artillery. On his way to destroy the railroad and canal complex at Lynchburg with 10,000 men, Maj. Gen. Franz Sigel was attacked by a makeshift force of 4,100 Confederates led by Maj. Gen. John C. Breckinridge. Among the Rebel forces were 257 VMI cadets, who were meant to be kept in reserve. In the heat of battle, however, the boys—whose average age was 15—were put on the front line. Five were killed and dozens wounded. (Five more later died from their wounds.) The students were able to hold the line for half an hour and capture a cannon, helping defeat the superior Union forces and earning themselves a place in Civil War legend.

Whether or not you think children in combat is something worth celebrating, the well-preserved battlefield (866/515-1864, www2.vmi.edu/museum/nm/index.html, 9 A.M.–5 P.M. daily, $10 adults, $6 children 6–12) is easily understood and absorbing. Inside the **Hall of Valor** run by VMI is a visitors center and a museum covering the entire Civil War. An Emmy-winning docudrama, shown on the hour, re-creates the battle using actors and historic images.

Pick up a walking-tour brochure and step outside to begin the mile-long loop trail. Imagine yourself as one of the students, your high spirits drenched by four days' marching in the rain. A headlong charge takes you through the buildings of the Bushong farm, where the terrified family hides in the basement, and across the mud-clogged "field of lost shoes" toward the deafening thunder of the Union guns.

A 200-foot vista over the peaceful Shenandoah River marks where the trail turns back. The cadets' role in the battle is honored in a formal ceremony every May 15 at VMI. The costumed reenactment of the battle and the cadets' charge is one of the oldest in the country, held around the same date.

Commercial Caves

North of New Market at I-81 exit 269, **Shenadoah Caverns** (540/477-3115 or 888/422-8376, www.shenandoahcaverns.com, tours 9 A.M.–6:15 P.M. daily, to 5:15 or 4:15 off-season, $22 adults, $10 children 6–14) were unearthed in 1884 during the construction of the valley railroad. Opened to the public in 1922, they're the only ones in the state with an elevator and feature flowstone slabs called the Bacon Formations as well as other formations. Your ticket includes admission to **Main Streets of Yesteryear,** a set of window displays filled with miniatures, and **American Celebrations on Parade,** a 40,000-square-foot exhibit of 50 years of parade floats from around the country.

The largest billboard in the eastern United States points off I-81 toward **Endless Caverns** (800/544-2283, www.endlesscavern.com, tours 9 A.M.–6 P.M. daily, to 4 P.M. off-season, $16 adults, $8 children 4–12), a serpentine network of passages and tunnels discovered in 1879 by two boys hunting a rabbit. Five miles have been mapped so far, with no end in sight, giving Endless Caverns the most untamed feel of any of Virginia's caves. New passageways are still being discovered, and they've even unearthed a mammoth tooth in here. Refreshments (including bottled cave water) are available in the 1920s limestone lodge, and 145 campsites ($40 and up) are available, some with full hookups.

Other Activities

New Market Walking Tours (www.new-market-virginia-walking-tours.com, $10 adults, $5 children) depart from the Apple Blossom Inn at 10:30 A.M. Monday–Saturday May–October, with some afternoon tours as well (call for details). Costumed guides leads visitors through the town's historic district and tell tales of Colonial times and the Civil War, as well as local folklore. Evening lantern tours are offered in October.

Shopping

A handful of antiques stores lines Congress Street within a few blocks of the center of town at Old Cross Road. Places such as **Shop Civil War** (9398 S. Congress St., 540/740-2729) stock everything from art and flags to real Civil War relics. Find functional and fine art pottery at **Art Studio Pottery** (346 Endless Caverns Rd., 540/896-4400, www.artstudio pottery.com).

Accommodations

One mile north of I-81 exit 264, you'll find **Quality Inn Shenandoah Valley** (162 W. Old Cross Rd., 540/740-3141, $80–100), offering a pool and the Johnny Appleseed Restaurant.

Dating to the end of the 18th century, the **Rosendale Inn** (17917 Farmhouse Ln., 540/740-4281, www.rosendaleinn.com) sits on 20 acres off Route 793 on the way to Endless Caverns. Four rooms and a separate guest cottage are $105–160, and there's a veranda with rocking chairs for enjoying the evening. The **Jacob Swartz House** (574 Jiggady Rd., 540/740-9208 or 877/740-9208, www.jacob swartz.com) can put up guests in a two-bedroom cottage with a living room, full kitchen, wood-burning stove, and screened porch set along a river bluff. Rates start at $125 single occupancy per night ($25 each extra adult/teen, $15 each child), including full breakfast. Enjoy an on-site therapeutic or aromatherapy massage as an add-on to your stay. Call for directions.

The **Cross Roads Inn Bed & Breakfast** (9222 John Sevier Rd., 540/740-4157 or 888/740-4157, www.crossroadsinnva.com, $75–135) was built in 1925 for Claude Hoover, one of the driving forces behind the creation of Shenandoah National Park. The late Victorian home has six rooms, several with whirlpool tubs and fireplaces, and beautifully landscaped grounds. It's at the intersection of Route 211 to Luray and John Sevier Road, just east of Route 11 north.

Rent the 1806 **Apple Blossom Inn** (9317 N. Congress St., 540/740-3747, www.apple blossominn.net, $135 d, $25 each extra person) in the Historic District and have it entirely to yourself: two bedrooms, a full kitchen, parlor, gardens, secret courtyard, and all. It holds up to four guests and comes with a country breakfast.

Campsites at the **Shenandoah Valley KOA** (12480 Mountain Valley Rd., 540/896-8929) in nearby Broadway, Virginia, are $35–55. It's 3.3 miles east of I-81 exit 257 on Route 608.

Food

With a real 1950s-diner feel, the **Southern Kitchen** (9576 S. Congress St., 540/740-3514, all meals daily) has sandwiches for $5–8 and dinners for $10–18. A big statue of the man himself marks the **Johnny Appleseed Restaurant** at the Quality Inn Shenandoah Valley (162 W. Old Cross Rd., 540/740-3141), serving home-style food daily for all meals. Homemade apple fritters and buttermilk biscuits from scratch are on the menu.

Information

Just off I-81 exit 264 is the **Shenandoah Valley Visitor Center** (277 W. Old Cross Rd., 540/740-3132, 9 A.M.–5 P.M. daily).

LURAY

The seat of Page County is best known for what it's near: the central entrance for Shenandoah National Park and the most impressive caverns in the East. The U.S. 211 bypass serves as Main Street, divided into east and west at Broad Street (U.S. 340).

◖ Luray Caverns

The most impressive of Virginia's commercial caves, this U.S. Registered Natural Landmark (540/743-6551, www.luraycaverns.com, 9 A.M.–7 P.M. daily, to 4 P.M. off-season, $21 adults, $10 children 6–12) encloses the most-visited caverns in the East. From the start, the ceilings bristle, the floors bulge, and the walls

Stalactites and stalagmites come in all shapes and sizes at Luray Caverns.

flow in a scale that makes you wish the tour lasted longer than an hour. Fifty-foot drapery (a type of rock formation that looks like curtains) is pulled so thin that some parts are translucent; nearly pure white calcite columns and a 170-ton fallen stalactite the size of a school bus are other highlights. Dream Lake, 2,500 feet square, is only 1–6 inches deep, with a reflection that's otherworldly.

The most famous feature of Luray Caverns, though, is only half natural: a "stalacpipe organ," which produces tones with electronically controlled rubber mallets striking stalactites to produce music that brings to mind a subterranean marimba—and somehow Tim Burton. Covering 312 acres, the organ is listed in Guinness World Records as the largest natural instrument in the world.

Back out in the fresh air is the Car and Carriage Caravan Museum (included in admission), with 140 models as old as 1625. No cavern resort complex would be complete without a garden maze ($6 adults, $5 children), gas station, airport, restaurant, golf course, and gift shop, selling everything from pottery to handcuffs.

A visit to the Car and Carriage Caravan Museum, replete with classic Model Ts, is included in admission for the Luray Caverns.

Other Diversions and Recreation

The **Luray Zoo** (540/743-4113, www.lurayzoo.com, 10 A.M.–5 P.M. daily, shorter hours in spring, fall, and winter, $10 adults, $5 children 3–12) is home to one of Virginia's largest scaly collections, both extinct and living. Cobras, alligators, and 20-foot pythons coexist with exotic birds and mammals along Route 211 one-half mile west of town, with live educational shows and a petting zoo for the children and batrachophobes. The zoo is a rescue zoo, meaning it specializes in serving as a home for unwanted, abused, or confiscated exotic animals. The owners are both licensed falconers and eager to talk about their high-flying pastime.

A carillon of 47 bells fills the **Luray Singing Tower** on West Main Street opposite the caverns. Free live concerts are given weekends in the spring and fall and during the week in summer.

The South Fork of the Shenandoah from Luray to Front Royal is known for great bass fishing, packing the placid waters with canoes, tubes, and private boats on busy weekend afternoons from spring to fall. **Shenandoah River Outfitters** (6502 S. Page Valley Rd./Rte. 684, 540/743-4159 or 800/622-6632, www.shenandoahriver.com) offers rentals and trips along the river 10 miles northwest of town. Beginning white-water rentals start at $55 for a two-person canoe and $36 for a kayak, or you can opt for an eight-mile flatwater float for the same price. Tube rentals and cookouts are only two of the other options. They also operate fully furnished log cabins ($100–150 d), a mountain cottage ($100–180; sleeps up to three), and campground ($8 pp).

Events

Luray's **Festival of Spring** in mid-May fills the streets with pony and llama rides, antiques dealers, and food vendors. A traditional maypole dance and historic home tours are also part of the festivities. This coincides with the New Market battle reenactment weekend. Taking place around Columbus Day in October, the **Page County Heritage Festival** has been known for arts and crafts since 1969. More than 10,000 people show up for the antique tractor and engine show, chili cook-off, and pony rides.

Accommodations

Rooms at the nearly identical **Luray Caverns Motel East** (831 W. Main St., 540/743-6551 or 888/941-4531) and **Luray Caverns Motel West** (U.S. 211 W., 540/743-6551 or 888/941-4531) range $72–94. **The Mimslyn** (401 W. Main St., 540/244-9445 or 800/296-5105,

---

SHENANDOAH AREA WINERIES

Barren Ridge Vineyards
984 Barren Ridge Rd., Fishersville
540/248-3300
www.barrenridgevineyards.com

Cave Ridge Vineyard
1476 Conicville Rd., Mt. Jackson
540/477-2585
www.caveridge.com

Crooked Run Cellars
1685 Crooked Run Rd., Mt. Jackson
540/477-9030
www.crookedruncellars.com

CrossKeys Vineyards
6011 E. Timber Ridge Rd., Mt. Crawford
540/234-0505
www.crosskeysvineyards.com

Lexington Valley Vineyard
80 Norton Way, Rockbridge Baths
540/462-2974
www.lexingtonvalleyvineyard.com

North Mountain Vineyard & Winery
4374 Swartz Rd., Maurertown
540/436-9463
www.northmountainvineyard.com

Rockbridge Vineyard
35 Hill View Ln., Raphine
888/511-9463
www.rockbridgevineyard.com

Shenandoah Vineyards
3659 S. Ox Rd., Edinburg
540/984-8699
www.shentel.net/shenvine

Veramar Vineyard
905 Quarry Rd., Berryville
540/955-5510
www.veramar.com

www.mimslyninn.com) opened in 1931 on top of a commanding hill just outside the center of town. Renovated in 2007, the "grand old inn of Virginia" still sits amid 14 acres of lawns and gardens overlooked by a terrace and solarium. from the front doors, a red carpet flows up the central staircase.

Rooms in **The Cardinal Inn** (1005 E. Main St., 540/743-5010 or 888/648-4633, www.luraybestvalueinn.com) are $50–80, and the hotel has a porch with a view of the mountains. Rates include continental breakfast.

The **Woodruff Inns** (330 Mechanic St., 540/743-1494, www.woodruffinns.com) are headquartered in **The Woodruff House,** an 1882 Fairytale Victorian, but there is also the **Victorian Rose,** an 1890 French Country Victorian, and a **cabin** and **cottage** along the riverfront. Room rates range $110–250 (the cottage and cabins are $160–250), with an additional charge for gourmet meals if you want them. Amenities include outdoor garden hot tubs, flower gardens, whirlpool tubs, and private balconies.

Under new management, **The Victorian Inn** (138 E. Main St., 540/860-4229, www.victorianinnluray.com) is an 1885 Fantasy Victorian building with three rooms priced $160–250.

Camping

Yogi Bear's Jellystone Park (540/743-4002 or 800/420-6679, www.campluray.com) is off Route 211 three miles east of town. Campsites are $35–57, and cabins range $90–160. On hand are a stocked fishing pond, two pools, camp store, and laundromat. **The Country Waye RV Resort** (3402 Kimball Rd., 888/765-7222, www.countrywaye.com, mid-Mar.–mid-Nov.) offers great views and 100 campsites for $20–30. All the amenities are included: pool, hot tub, game room, laundry, and even an Internet café. Maintained by the National Forest, **Camp Roosevelt** (540/984-4101) has 10 basic sites for $10 each, 8.5 miles northwest of Luray on Route 675.

Food

On Luray's Main Street, the **Artisans Grill** (2 E. Main St., 540/743-7030, lunch and dinner Wed.–Mon.) serves art-themed sandwiches ($6–7), soups, and salads ganic produce. Dinner sp stuffed portobello mush by-back ribs. Sticking v an on-site gallery shov tional artists and 7–9 r. sicians strum Eagles and James

Just up the street, **A Moment to Remem** (55 E. Main St., 540/743-1121, breakfast and lunch Mon.–Sat., dinner Thurs.–Sat., brunch Sun.) is both a casual restaurant serving German and American cuisine and an espresso bar. Owners and husband and wife John and Elke Thomas know their schnitzel—Elke hails from Germany, and John spent eight years there. The two met in Elke's previous German restaurant, 25 miles north in Front Royal. Deli sandwiches and paninis go for $5–8 at lunch, and dinner dishes, such as a bratwurst sampler, run $13–17.

Swing by **Main Street Bakery** (127 E. Main St., 540/743-6909) for cinnamon-raisin bread warm from the oven, served with a generous pat of butter. The bakery is open for breakfast and lunch Tuesday–Saturday, and serves vegan baked goods, too.

The Farmhouse Restaurant (326 Hawksbill Park Rd., 540/778-2285 or 888/418-7000, www.jordanhollow.com, all meals daily) at the Jordan Hollow Inn in nearby Stanley is the area's most acclaimed eatery. Featured on the Food Network and in *Bon Appetit,* the restaurant offers gourmet breakfasts, a full bar, and excellent entrées like chicken marsala and Virginia ham steak with wild mushrooms for $18–32 at dinner. Two of the four dining rooms are in a 200-year-old log farmhouse.

Information

For information on festivals and other activities in town, contact the **Luray-Page County Chamber of Commerce** (18 Campbell St., 540/743-3915 or 888/743-3915, www.luraypage.com), which also operates a visitors center 9 A.M.–5 P.M. daily.

Sperryville

The mid-Atlantic's most famous hike goes by a funny name, Old Rag—as in "Old Ragged

..." The popularity of this rocky ... is hard to exaggerate. You can even ... Christmas ornament to commemorate ... hike. While Old Rag falls within the jurisdiction of Shenandoah National Park, it sits a short distance from the Blue Ridge near the tiny hamlet of Sperryville. To get to the trailhead, you (and a myriad of other hikers) must pass through town, where a number of cafés and shops line the petite Main Street.

If you can freshen up after hiking, go to **Thornton River Grille** (3710 Sperryville Pike, 540/987-8790, www.thorntonrivergrille.com, lunch and dinner Tues.–Sat., brunch Sun.), a place that Luray residents will cross the mountains to visit for special occasions. Items such as grilled rib eye with sautéed mushrooms and a house-ground cheeseburger on a challah roll go for $13–29 (lunch is $9–14).

Shenandoah National Park

One of the country's most popular national parks protects nearly 300 square miles of the Blue Ridge Mountains, from some 60 rough-edged peaks to the stream-filled nooks and wildflower-dotted crannies in between. Zipping it all together is the Skyline Drive, stretching for 105 miles along ridgetops from Front Royal to Waynesboro. Arguably the most beautiful drive in the eastern United States, this meandering byway continues as the Blue Ridge Parkway south toward North Carolina and Great Smoky Mountains National Park.

Few visitors venture far off the road, either because they're content with the countless overlooks or because they're in a hurry to move on. Those who do leave their cars discover gushing spring waterfalls, quiet wooded glades, and mountaintop views that often beat anything available from the road. It takes little effort to put space between you and the asphalt, and you won't be disappointed.

All mileposts (mp) are measured from 0 at Front Royal.

The 105 miles of Skyline Drive stretch from Front Royal to Waynesboro.

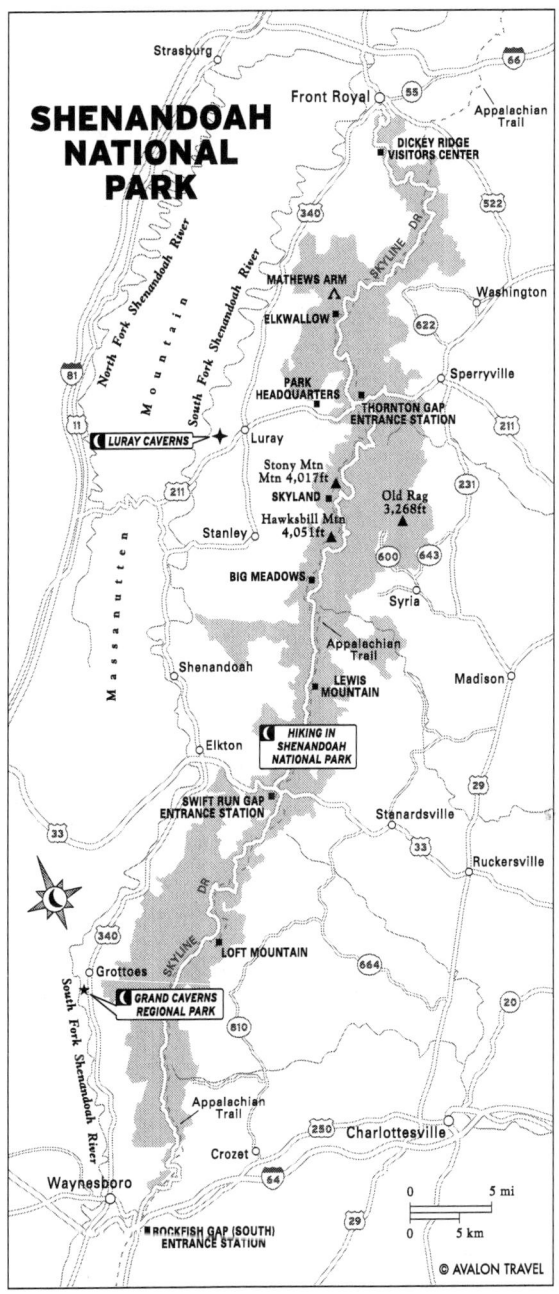

HISTORY

The idea of protecting a large swath of Virginia's mountains had been around since the turn of the 20th century, but it took governor Harry Byrd's creation of a state conservation and development commission in 1926 to get the ball rolling. Without federal money to buy land, the Virginia state legislature passed an act that required landowners to sell their plots within 10 years. The project received the enthusiastic support of President Hoover, who spent every moment he could spare at a fishing camp on the upper Rapidan River within the borders of the proposed park.

Ground was broken for the Skyline Drive in 1931, supposedly after Hoover got the idea during a horseback ride along the crest of the mountains. In 1933, president Franklin Roosevelt's Civilian Conservation Corps pitched in with the construction of sturdy scenic overlooks, picnic areas, and landscaping. More than a thousand mountain residents were compelled to find somewhere else to live by the time the park was dedicated in 1936. The road was finished three years later, and the land was returned to its natural state. In 1976, Congress declared two-fifths of the park (more than 79,000 acres) wilderness.

HABITATS

Shenandoah National Park straddles the mid-Atlantic transition between the Northern and Southern Appalachian ecosystems, giving it an incredible variety of plant and animal life.

Flora

With elevations ranging from 600 feet at the northern entrance to more than 4,000 feet on mountain peaks, Shenandoah National Park encloses a constantly changing deciduous forest. More than 95 percent of the park is forested now with close to 100 tree species and 47 species of mosses and ferns. The chestnut blight near the turn of the 20th century wiped out most of that native species. Oaks and hickories are among the most common trees in the park today. Mixed hardwood forests in the middle elevation include birch and maples. Pines and scrub oak grow on drier slopes, while ash, basswood, and yellow poplar line many streams. The forests explode into brilliant color in autumn, peaking around mid-October. The National Park Service posts weekly foliage reports and live images from a "leaf cam" in autumn so you can time your visit accordingly (www.nps.gov/shen/parknews/fall_colors.htm).

Azaleas and mountain laurel fill the understory; the latter blooms pink in June. Huckleberries, blueberries, and blackberries ripen in mid- to late summer, attracting animals on two and four legs. At the right time of year the park sparkles with over 1,000 species of wildflowers, especially along Skyline Drive and in Big Meadows. Higher elevations help the spring blossoms of violets, chickweeds, and bloodroots persist after summer heat has claimed the Piedmont. (Look along low-elevation streams for more spring blooms.) Periwinkles, pink ladyslippers, trillium, and geraniums flower close behind, followed by gaudy yellow cowslips in May, touch-me-nots in June, and black-eyed Susans and Queen

THE APPALACHIAN TRAIL STORY

Classic though it is, the Appalachian Trail has a relatively short history. The "impossible" idea began as a 1921 proposal by Massachusetts regional planner Benton MacKaye, who envisioned it as an escape for residents of the increasingly populated East. (Today close to two-thirds of the population of the United States lives within 500 miles of the trail.) The Appalachian Trail Conference (now the Appalachian Trail Conservancy), a loose organization of local hiking clubs, was formed in 1925. Thanks to its unpaid efforts, the first continuous trail opened in 1937, but various highways, extreme weather, and the privations of World War II almost buried the project. In the early 1950s, the entire pathway was again cleared and re-marked, and in 1968 it was declared the nation's first National Scenic Trail, akin to a linear National Park but without the funding.

At its northern end, the trail starts at the peak of Maine's Mt. Katahdin (5,267 ft.), winding its most isolated miles through the Maine backwoods. From there it passes through the White Mountains of New Hampshire and the Green Mountains of Vermont before clipping off the western ends of Massachusetts and Connecticut. Southern New York state, where the trail crosses the Hudson River, marks the beginning of the trail's least rural section. Northern New Jersey is next, followed by the Cumberland Valley in eastern Pennsylvania. Eventually the ATC headquarters in Harpers Ferry, West Virginia, comes into sight, where thru-hikers sign a logbook and have their pictures taken.

Virginia contains a quarter of the AT and some of its most breathtaking scenery. Winding down around the Skyline Drive through Shenandoah National Park, the trail then steers west to touch the West Virginia line. It crosses the Blue Ridge Parkway nine times on its way through some of the state's most beautiful wilderness, including the Mount Rogers National Recreation Area. South of Virginia, the AT follows the state line between Tennessee and North Carolina on its way through the rugged undulations of the Great Smoky Mountains National Park. The finish line (or starting point, if you're heading north) comes at the peak of Springer Mountain (3,782 ft.) in Georgia's Chattahoochee National Forest.

Anne's lace in August, when sunflowers also reach their peak.

Fauna

More than 50 species of mammals call the park home. You may spot squirrels, raccoons, and a trundling opossum or groundhog. A few lucky hikers may see a bobcat or gray fox among the trees. At dawn and dusk, white-tailed deer congregate in open areas, particularly Big Meadows, browsing on tender plants until spooked by a car or breeze. A few colonies of beavers have reestablished themselves along the Thornton and Rapidan Rivers. Shenandoah National Park has one of the highest densities of black bears of any park in the country—about one per square mile. In a terrifying moment, our dog once chased one from a tree! (Do follow the leash laws in the park—trust us, it's worth it.) Bear boxes and proper food storage are a must if camping or backpacking.

Two hundred species of birds include permanent residents such as the barred owl, ruffed grouse, and wild turkey. Migratory woodcocks arrive in the early spring, while warblers, thrushes, tanagers, and flycatchers move in during the summer. A hawk or six-foot turkey vulture circling the updrafts is a common sight along the Skyline Drive. Virginia's first breeding pair of peregrine falcons in 40 years was found nesting in the park in 1994.

ACCESS

Shenandoah National Park is divided into three sections by roads bisecting the Skyline Drive. The Northern District stretches from the entrance station at Front Royal (U.S. 340, mp 0) to Thornton Gap (mp 31.5), where U.S. 211 connects Luray to the Piedmont. The Central District continues south to Swift Run Gap (mp 65.5), where U.S. 33 crosses the park as it runs to Harrisonburg. Rockfish Gap (mp 104.6) marks the boundary of the Southern District and the Skyline Drive, with access to I-64 and U.S. 250.

Each entrance has an information booth where you can pay your admission fee and receive a map of the park and, in summer and fall, a copy of the *Shenandoah Overlook* visitor guide. Various hiking trails enter the park from the base of the mountains on either side, often continuing as far as the crest and the Skyline Drive.

Fees

Shenandoah National Park's early years—when it cost a quarter to enter and a buck for an annual pass—are long gone. In the mid-1990s, national park fees were raised throughout the country in an effort to make up for chronic underfunding and to direct more dollars back into the parks. Today, entrance to the park costs $15 per car ($10 Dec.–Feb.) and $8 per pedestrian or bicyclist ($5 Dec.–Feb.); the pass is good for seven consecutive days.

A year-long pass good for any federal recreation site that charges admission is $80. U.S. citizens over age 62 can buy a senior pass ($10), and visitors with disabilities can receive a free access pass with similar privileges. Fees in all national parks are suspended the last Saturday in September for National Public Lands Day.

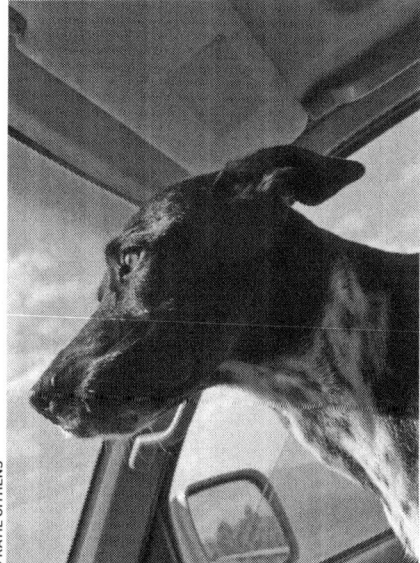

Dogs eagerly anticipate a trip to Shenandoah National Park, but they must be leashed at all times.

When to Go

For the height of the fall foliage display in October, you'll probably have to make accommodation reservations—sometimes as much as a year in advance. The best time to avoid the million or so people who visit per year, then, while still getting the view, vegetation, and wildlife you came for, is in the spring and on weekdays during the summer and fall. In the winter, all facilities shut down and parts of the Skyline Drive are often closed due to inclement weather. Then you'll have most of the park to yourself, which can be a magical experience if you're prepared. Bring a full tank of gas, tire chains or snow tires, water, and warm clothing, and call ahead for conditions.

◖ HIKING

Over 500 miles of trails crisscross the park. City softies beware: They're most often uphill or downhill, and occasionally precipitous. More than a dozen waterfalls accessible only on foot are a highlight of any sweaty ramble, as are the pools below and in between. Remnants of former homesites are visible in crumbling walls and chimneys and mossy cemeteries hidden in the underbrush.

Each visitors center has trail maps, along with topographical maps and detailed maps of the entire park. Various trail guides are available at the bookstore in the park visitors centers. **Pets** are allowed on most trails, but only on leashes; ask at the visitors centers about which trails are off-limits. **Bicycles** are only allowed on Skyline Drive and other paved areas—but wow, what a scenic cycling route even so.

A 101-mile segment of the **Appalachian Trail** threads its way along Skyline Drive, making it ideal for short hikes as it crosses and re-crosses the road. Many loop trails include part of the AT.

Listed here, by difficulty from north to south, is just a sample of the park's plethora of trails.

Easy Hikes

A self-guided walk on the **Fox Hollow Trail** starts at mile 4.5, passing an old homesite and cemetery in a 1.2-mile circuit. Another short self-guided trail, the **Stony Man Trail,** climbs the second-highest peak in the park from Skyland Resort (mp 42). Also near Skyland, the 1.2-mile **Limberlost Trail** heads past laurel bushes and evergreens. A crushed greenstone walkway makes it the first and only fully ADA-accessible trail in the park.

Near milepost 51 spreads **Big Meadows,** the largest treeless area in the park. These 135 acres of fields and wetlands make up one of the most popular destinations along the Skyline Drive, offering various visitor facilities and a good chance of spotting herds of deer that are unimpressed by cars or people. Trails lead to different waterfalls, including the popular **Dark Hollow Falls,** a 70-foot flow over green volcanic stone (1.4 miles round-trip). Or, head down the 1.8-mile **Story of the Forest Trail.**

Toward the southern end of the park, the **North Fork of Moormans River** bears the scars of a catastrophic flood in June 1995 following six straight days of rain in the park. It's still a beautiful walk along the river, although

© KATIE GITHENS

A hike up Old Rag is an all-hands-and-feet endeavor with narrow passageways and the occasional rock scramble along the way.

EXODUS OF THE MOUNTAIN PEOPLE

Hiking in the "wilderness" of Shenandoah National Park, you might be startled to stumble across an old cemetery overgrown with underbrush or the foundation of a derelict cabin. What is a cemetery doing in a national park? It was there first, as it turns out.

For all the National Park Service literature about how the New Deal and the Civil Conservation Corps shaped Shenandoah National Park as we see it today, far less has been published about the 500 or more families forced to relocate for its creation. Congress approved creating the park in 1926, prompting alarm and a letter-writing campaign among the literate living in the mountain hollows.

Skyline Drive was already under construction when Arno Cammerer, director of the parks service, officially announced in 1934 that the federal government would require residents to vacate the Blue Ridge. His policy decision drew few questions from outside Appalachia, given a widely held perception that the mountain people were barefoot hillbillies, backwards and "disreputable" to begin with (the cottage industry of moonshining had something to do with this reputation).

While some Blue Ridge families left willingly, even happily, others went down swinging, particularly tenant farmers who received no payment for leaving the land since they were not the landowners, and landowners who felt the government had undervalued their land. "Time and again we were threatened with sudden death by infuriated landowners," said William Carson, chairman of the state agency charged with handling the legalities of acquiring parkland. All told, the national park comprises more than 3,000 individual tracts of land bought or condemned under eminent domain in the 1930s.

Vacated homes were then demolished in an effort to return the land to its natural, pre-human state as quickly as possible, with few exceptions. Even so, the observant hiker can still run across lasting artifacts of these Appalachian communities. For a vintage photo gallery of mountain residents before their exodus into the valley, see the National Park Service website (www.nps.gov/shen/historyculture/mtnresidents.htm).

---

the footing can get tricky at times. It's a little over 1.5 miles upstream to Big Branch, which spills in from the left (west). Park officials estimate that, for a time, there was as much water rushing in here as spills over Great Falls on the Potomac at low flow. The river has begun to recover well, and there are many spots to take a dip or fish along the way. The trail starts at the park boundary and leads outside the park. Reach the trailhead by taking Route 614 upriver from Route 810, north of Crozet. Up and back, the hike should take about three hours.

Moderate Hikes

If solitude is what you're after, head to **Jeremy's Run,** a beautiful stream valley full of luxuriant forests, waterfalls, and pools. It's a six-mile round-trip hike down and back up, and it's steep in spots. Combined with an ascent of **Knob Mountain,** this makes a modestly challenging 12-mile loop from Elkwallow Picnic Area (mp 24). From the lower section of the picnic area, follow the brown Jeremy's Run trail marker. Be ready to cross the stream numerous times.

Just south of Skyland Resort, you'll find the parking lot and trailhead for **White Oak Canyon** (mp 42.6), a spectacular (and popular) hike down a steep gorge past pools, huge boulders, and six waterfalls ranging 35–85 feet high. The 1,000-foot climb to the first waterfall is steep. It connects with the **Limberlost Trail,** where you'll find old-growth hemlocks.

At mile 52.5, the **Mill Prong Trail** leads downhill to Rapidan Camp, President Hoover's weekend White House, which was donated to the proposed park in 1933. From the South River Picnic Area (mp 62.8), a trail leads to **South River Falls,** the third highest in the park at the head of a steep gorge. You'll climb 850 feet in 2.6 miles round-trip.

Near mile 90, the 6.8-mile **Riprap Hollow Trail** offers great views and access to one of the park's largest swimming holes. Include Calvary Rock, Chimney Rock, the Wildcat Ridge Trail, and the AT to make it a 9.8-mile circuit hike, bedecked with mountain laurel blossoms in the spring.

Strenuous Hikes

The trail to **Old Rag Mountain** begins at a parking lot on Route 600, which leaves Route 231 between Sperryville and Madison to the east of the park. The 7.2-mile circuit winds up, over, and around a huge jumble of granite boulders to the peak (3,291 ft.), dotted with water-filled depressions called "buzzard baths." As you enjoy the view, think about the fact that the rock you're standing on is thought to be some of the oldest exposed rock on the East Coast—around 1.1 billion years old. Return via the Weakley Hollow Fire Road.

Because it's one of the more spectacular hikes within day-trip distance of Washington, D.C., Old Rag is popular, and it can get staggeringly crowded on sunny weekends.

A great alternative to Old Rag, especially when the crowds are plentiful, is the 6.1-mile loop to the top of **Robertson Mountain.** It's also a strenuous climb, but after passing through peaceful Corbin Hollow and following a wonderful trout stream, you're rewarded with views that are easily comparable—you can even see Old Rag from the top. Park in the same place as Old Rag, but take the Weakley Hollow Fire Road up to the trailhead. (Combine with Old Rag to make a 12-mile trek that climbs 4,000 feet.)

A steep path leaves from Hawksbill Gap (mp 45.6) to the top of **Hawksbill Mountain** (4,049 ft.), the highest point in the park. Climbing 1,557 feet in less than one mile, the trail reaches an observation point at the peak, a great place to spot hawks.

ACCOMMODATIONS, CAMPING, AND SERVICES

Information and reservations for Big Meadows Lodge, Skyland Resort, and the Lewis Mountain Cabins can be obtained from **Aramark** (888/896-3833, www.visitshenandoah.com). Prices are highest in October, and a few different lodging and dining packages

Unlike most of Virginia's peaks in the Blue Ridge Mountains, Old Rag has a bald summit.

are available. Gasoline, oil, air, water, groceries, and camping supplies are available at all three waysides (Elkwallow, Big Meadow, and Loft Mountain).

The park's four main campgrounds are open spring through fall and feature roomy tent, trailer, and RV sites (no water or electric hookups) with picnic tables and grills for $14–19. The Potomac Appalachian Trail Club (703/242-0693, www.patc.net) maintains six primitive cabins with mattresses and pit toilets ($25–40). Backcountry camping is free, but you'll need a permit from one of the visitors centers, entrance stations, or park headquarters (also available by mail). Facilities start opening in March or April and start closing from October to late November, so call ahead if you plan to visit at either end of the season.

Starting from Front Royal, the **Mathews Arm Campground** at mile 22.1 has 179 sites and is near the trailhead for Overall Run Falls, the tallest waterfall in the park. **Elkwallow Wayside** (mp 24.1) has a snack bar, camp store, gas station, and gift shop. **Skyland Resort** (mp 41.8) began as Stony Man Camp in 1894. At 3,680 feet, it's the highest point on Skyline Drive, which means great views from most of the 179 rooms. "Rustic" cabin rooms are $106–250, motel-style rooms in the main lodge range $125–160, and suites are $160–220. Family cabins with room to sleep six to eight people are $250. (Prices are slightly higher in October.) None have phones, but some have TVs. The glass-walled restaurant lets you enjoy steaks, trout, and other basic fare while looking out over the forest, and the Tap Room has live entertainment on summer nights. Guided horseback and pony rides are available from the stables.

Built in 1939, the **Big Meadows Lodge** has a cozier feel, thanks to stone walls paneled with native chestnut wood. The sitting room features a fireplace and outdoor deck with the requisite gorgeous vista; otherwise, the facilities are similar to those at Skyland. Rooms in the main lodge are $106–160, cabins are about $100, and suites $160. At the same turn-off (mp 51.2) is the park's largest and most popular campground with 217 sites. You can reserve sites in advance (reservations are required between mid-May and November) by calling 877/444-6777. Next to the Byrd Visitors Center is the Big Meadows Wayside with a restaurant, gift shop, camp store, and gas station.

Lewis Mountain (mp 57.5) has cabins with one or two rooms for $106. All cabins are heated and linens are provided, but they don't have phones or TVs. Cooking is done outdoors on a grill. Tent cabins are also available for $30. Thirty-one campsites ($15) are offered first-come, first-served, right next to the information center, gift and food shop, showers, and laundry. At **Loft Mountain** (mp 80), you'll find the Loft Mountain Wayside gift shop and snack bar. More than 200 campsites are available mostly on a first-come, first-served basis, with a camp store, shower, and laundry.

Guided outdoor adventure programs, including hiking and rock climbing, are offered April–November for about $75. See www.visitshenandoah.com for more details.

INFORMATION
Maps and Information

The Potomac Appalachian Trail Club sells three topographical maps (numbers 9, 10, and 11) covering the entire park. The 1:75,000-scale map by National Geographic's **Trails Illustrated** (www.trailsillustrated.com) is printed on tearproof plastic for $12; get map number 228. More detailed quadrangle maps are available from the U.S. Geological Survey (USGS) information line (888/275-8747, http://topomaps.usgs.gov). Park visitors centers and most local outfitters sell these maps.

The nonprofit **Shenandoah Natural Park Association** (540/999-3582, www.snpbooks.org) offers a large selection of books and other items, whose sales help support the park's interpretation and education efforts.

The website **Hiking Upward** (www.hikingupward.org) has great local hiking suggestions and resources.

Visitors Centers and Entrance Stations

The park has two visitors centers: The **Dickey Ridge Visitors Center** is at mile 4.6, and the **Harry F. Byrd Sr. Visitors Center** is in Big Meadows at milepost 51. They are both open 8:30 A.M.–5 P.M. daily April–late November, with reduced hours in April and November, and are stocked with information, films, exhibits, maps, and books. The **Loft Mountain Information Center** at mile 79.5 is also open on weekends. There are **entrance stations** at Front Royal and Rockfish Gap at either end of the park and at Thornton Gap (mp 31.5) and Swift Run Gap (mp 65.5).

Park Headquarters (540/999-3500, www.nps.gov/shen, 8 A.M.–4:30 P.M. Mon.–Fri.) is four miles east of Luray on U.S. 211.

Harrisonburg and Vicinity

The urban center of the northern Blue Ridge is home to 40,000 people and some 20 major industries. Thousands of local farmers come together in huge farmers markets, where you might find yourself parked next to a black horse-drawn buggy; about 1,000 Old Order Mennonites live in the area in a simple lifestyle similar to Pennsylvania's Amish, with whom they share a common Anabaptist religious heritage.

A strong arts presence complements three of the Shenandoah's largest schools—James Madison University (JMU), Bridgewater College, and Eastern Mennonite University—which have campuses in or near the city. Harrisonburg also excels in outdoor options, sandwiched as it is between Shenandoah National Park and the mountains of West Virginia, with lots of nearby rivers, lakes, and caverns to explore.

History

Harrisonburg was founded in the 1740s by Thomas Harrison near the intersection of the Spotswood Trail and the main Indian road down the valley. Strict Methodists started the city's first school in 1794, outlawing gaming and "instruments of music" and decreeing that no student be "permitted on any account whatever to wear Ruffles or powder his hair." The Battle of Harrisonburg, on June 6, 1862, saw the death of Gen. Turner Ashby, one of Stonewall Jackson's most trusted and respected officers.

Today, surrounding Rockingham County leads the state in production of beef, dairy

GHOSTS OF HARRISONBURG

On December 1, 1900, an aunt was checking on a baby in an upstairs bedroom when she bent to blow out an oil lamp. Low on oil, the lamp suddenly exploded, igniting the woman's dress and burning her so badly that she died the next day. Local legend holds that glowing handprints from the unlucky aunt appear on the wall of the old house, now part of the Willow Hill subdivision. Previous owners have witnessed the door to the master bedroom slamming shut on its own.

Residents of the Funk House on Mason Street – usually college students – tell of blasts of cold air gusting through rooms and doors closing without visible assistance. One person reported in the early 1970s that she woke up in the middle of the night feeling as if she were suffocating and couldn't get out of bed. Folklore scholars point out the old English custom of "mattressing," in which poor families piled mattresses on sick or elderly people they couldn't afford to take care of and sat on them until they suffocated.

Harrisonburg's most famous specter is said to be Colonel Warren, of the Warren-Sipe House, killed during the Battle of the Wilderness by a bullet in the head. Several witnesses have spotted his ghost at the first landing of the stairway, standing in full uniform with its head wrapped in wide bandages.

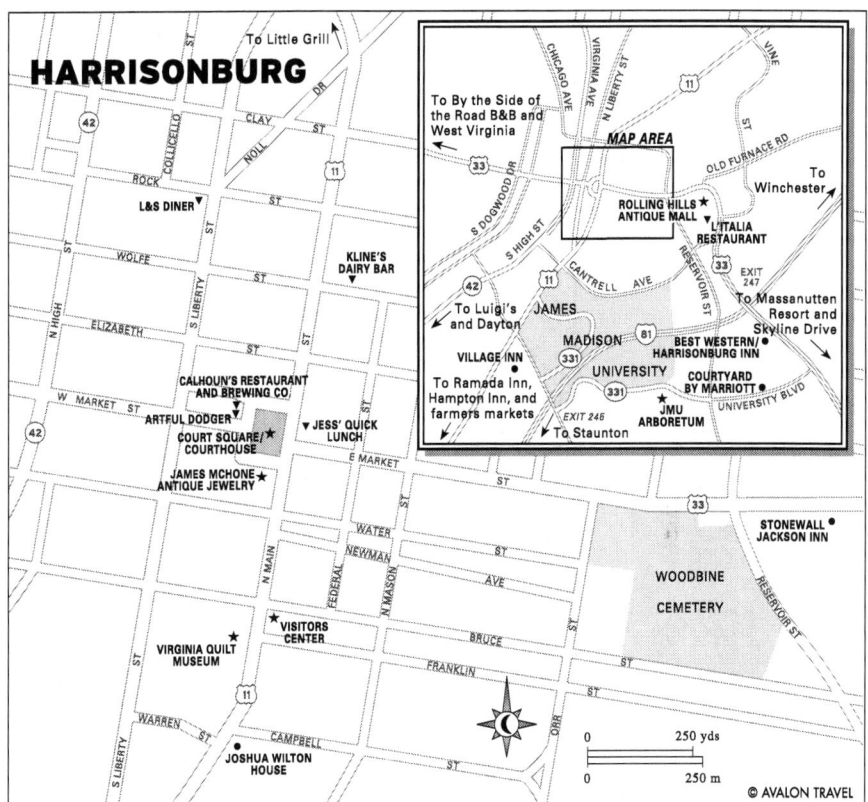

products, and poultry. Along with Staunton, Harrisonburg is a performing-arts hot spot of the Shenandoah, home to the Blue Ridge Theater Festival, the Court Square Theater, and the Valley Playhouse.

SIGHTS
Court Square

The heart of downtown rings the limestone-faced Rockingham County Courthouse. Dating to the turn of the 20th century, the imposing building is the fifth to sit on the original 1.5-acre plot of land donated by Thomas Harrison in 1779. Look for the round copper dome of the **springhouse** at the southwest corner, an exact replica, erected in 1995, of the original watering hole and meeting place.

Virginia Quilt Museum

Both traditional and modern masters of the art of quilting have works on display in the 1855 Warren-Sipe House (301 S. Main St., 540/433-3818, www.vaquiltmuseum.org, 10 A.M.–4 P.M. Tues.–Sat., $5 adults, $3 students 12–18, $2 children 6–12). People originally began making blanket covers from scraps out of necessity, because new bedclothes were expensive, but quilting has since evolved into its own art form. Rotating exhibits feature some wild, colorful examples edging toward fabric impressionism—notice the one made from old Bull Durham tobacco pouches.

James Madison University

This beautiful 696-acre campus is home to

17,000 students working towards a bachelor's or master's degree in the sciences, arts, business, health, or education. The well-rounded public university (540/568-6211, www.jmu.edu) is consistently cited by national publications as one of the top regional public institutions of higher learning. JMU also supports several successful sports teams that make regular appearances in the NCAA playoffs.

The gently sloping, grassy quadrangle is the perfect place for reading in the shade, Frisbee-throwing, or just taking a quiet stroll around this focal point of campus. The gracious red-roofed bluestone dormitory, classroom, and administration buildings, including the always-reliable Wilson Hall clock tower, constitute the original campus of the State Normal School for Women, a teachers' college founded in 1908.

At the other end of the spectrum, the **College of Integrated Science and Technology (CISAT)**—the first and most challenging curriculum of its kind—on the other side of I-81 is a modern marvel that is now the highest point in town (students call it the Emerald City). Sunset-watching is terrific from the parking lot outside the main building.

JMU administers the **Edith J. Carrier Arboretum** (540/568-3194, www.jmu.edu/arboretum) on University Boulevard. One hundred twenty-five acres of mature natural forest surround ponds and landscaped plots of shrubs and flowers. Nature trails weave through the leaves and across little Monet bridges over a stream. It's open dawn to dusk for free, with lectures, workshops, and tours offered 8 A.M.–4 P.M. Monday–Friday by prior appointment.

ENTERTAINMENT

Located in the same indoor plaza as Cally's restaurant, the **Court Square Theater** (61 Graham St., 540/433-9189, www.courtsquaretheater.com) operates under the auspices of the Arts Council of the Valley to bring theater, dance, movies, and live music to town. Call or check its website for a performance schedule.

JMU's **Masterpiece Theater** series (540/568-7000 or 877/201-7543, www.jmu.edu/cvpa/masterpiece) encompasses music, theater, and dance.

Tickets to **JMU Dukes** football and basketball games can be ordered from the JMU Athletic Ticket Office (540/568-3853, www.jmusports.com).

A wide variety of music acts perform at **The Pub** (1950 Deyerle Ave., 540/432-0610, www.dothepub.com), open until 2 A.M. daily.

SHOPPING

A Touch of the Earth (66 E. Market St., 540/432-1894) stocks a little bit of everything from far-off corners of the planet. Afghan carpets, Southwestern Indian pottery, Balinese carvings, and a roomful of drums are only the beginning. If you can't find something there, swing by **Gift & Thrift** (731 Mt. Clinton Pike, 540/433-8844, www.giftandthrift.org), covering the rest of the globe with Salvadoran painted boxes, Vietnamese ceramics, and Philippine shell ornaments. Half thrift shop and half international crafts store, this fascinating place is run by the Mennonites as a nonprofit organization.

James McHone Jewelry (75 S. Court Square, 540/433-1833) specializes in estate jewelry both new and antique. Harrisonburg artists' cooperative **Oasis** (103 S. Main St., 540/442-8188) stocks paintings, jewelry, furniture, photography, and pottery. Sixty dealers fill the **Rolling Hills Antique Mall** (779 E. Market St., 540/433-8988), stuffed to the rafters with everything from kitchen collectibles to automobilia.

On Saturday mornings year-round, as well as Tuesday mornings April–November, the **Harrisonburg Farmers Market** (540/476-3377, www.harrisonburgfarmersmarket.com) features fresh produce, baked goods, flowers, and greenery in the Turner Pavilion in the municipal parking lot at South Liberty and West Water Streets.

EVENTS

The Rockingham County Fairgrounds hosts the **Annual Memorial Day Horse Fair and Auction** in late May. In June, Eastern

Mennonite University rings with the sounds of classical music during the **Shenandoah Valley Bach Festival** (540/432-4367, www.emu.edu/bach).

Biggest of all is the **Rockingham County Fair** (www.rockinghamcountyfair.com) in August, an agricultural expo rated as one of the top 10 in the country by the *Los Angeles Times*. Competitions in flowers, crops, livestock, and art compete with country music, tractor pulls, and demolition derbies for a week near the middle of the month.

ACCOMMODATIONS
$50-100
The Village Inn (4979 S. Valley Pike/U.S. 11, 800/736-7355, $75–100) has been family owned and operated since 1936. It has an outdoor pool, and many rooms have outdoor decks. The **Ramada Inn** (1 Pleasant Valley Rd., 540/434-9981, $70–90) is off I-81 exit 243, with an outdoor pool and restaurant. Also try the **Best Western Harrisonburg Inn** (45 Burgess Rd., 540/433-6089, $80).

$100-150
◀ **The Joshua Wilton House** (412 S. Main St., 540/434-4464 or 888/294-5866, www.joshuawilton.com, $145–160, $85 corporate rates available midweek) vies for the titles of most elegant hotel and most elegant restaurant in the city. The Victorian mansion was built in 1888 by the owner of a hardware store on Court Square, who went on to start the local electric company. Wilton's residence, naturally, was the first in town with electricity—even before it had plumbing.

Much of the original materials and craftsmanship remain, including the leaded glass in the front door and the parquet floor and banister in the main hall, which even survived the house being used as a fraternity house for several years in the mid-1900s. Five bedrooms feature period antiques, four-poster beds, and faux-marble fireplaces. Enjoy the inn's award-winning cuisine, whipped up from locally sourced ingredients, in the two front rooms. More casual fare is served in three back rooms and on an outdoor patio café, with appetizers like Prince Edward Island mussels and entrées such as horseradish-crusted filet mignon. Rates include a gourmet breakfast in the sunroom.

Other good options in this price range include the **Hampton Inn** (43 Covenant Dr., 540/437-0090, $110–150) and a **Courtyard by Marriott** (1890 Evelyn Byrd Ave., 540/432-3031, $130–150).

$150-200
By the Side of the Road B&B (491 Garber's Church Rd., 540/801-0430 or 866/274-4887, www.bythesideoftheroad.com, $150–200) fills a Revolutionary-era Flemish bond building two miles to the east of downtown. It served as a hospital during the Civil War, during which Union soldiers tried to set fire to the foundation three times, unsuccessfully. Four suites in the main house and three separate cottages ($220–280) each have whirlpool tubs and breakfast delivered every morning.

The **Stonewall Jackson Inn** (547 E. Market St., 540/433-8233 or 800/445-5330, www.stonewalljacksoninn.com) near Old Town offers ten guest rooms ($130–180) named after Civil War figures. The restored circa-1885 mansion blends Queen Anne and New England cottage architecture. Enjoy a breakfast of crab soufflé or eggs Nova Scotia on the back porch.

FOOD
Snacks and Cafés
Retro couches, knickknacks, Wi-Fi, and local art on the walls make **The Artful Dodger** (47 W. Court Square, 540/432-1179, 8 A.M.–2 A.M. daily) a classic coffeehouse hip enough to make up for the lack of funk elsewhere in town. It also serves desserts and sandwiches ($5–7), and doubles as a cocktail lounge at night.

Look for the 20-foot ice cream cone in front of **Kline's Dairy Bar** (58 E. Wolfe St., 540/434-6980), where soft-serve ice cream, sundaes, and shakes have been served from the same Electro Freeze machine since 1943. Packed on weekend evenings in the summer, Kline's is so popular it has opened a second branch at 2425 South Main Street (540/434-4014), plus a third in Staunton and a fourth in Waynesboro.

The food at the quirky worker-owned **Little Grill Collective** (621 N. Main St., 540/434-3594, all meals Tues.–Sat., brunch Sun.) is healthy, inexpensive, and plentiful for the student-budget prices: mostly vegetarian and Mexican fare for $4–9. It's been operated as a restaurant since the 1940s and hosts live music at night. Cash only.

Casual

Jess' Quick Lunch (22 S. Main St., 540/434-8282) is an old city standby serving shakes, hamburgers, and the best hot dogs in town (three college students once ate 53 at a sitting). Low-priced breakfast, lunch, and dinner (hardly anything is more than $5) are served in diner booths and at the counter 9 A.M.–10 P.M. every day of the year.

"Home cooking from scratch" is the calling card of the bright-red **L&S Diner** (255 N. Liberty St., 540/801-0110), started in 1947 and with counter seating only for three inexpensive ($6 and under) meals Monday–Saturday.

Cally's Restaurant and Brewing Co. (41 Court Square, 540/434-8777, lunch and dinner daily) is a microbrewery popular with college students. It offers fresh beers brewed on-site, sandwiches ($7–10), and entrées ($14–19) ranging from pasta to seafood in a lively setting. A filling Sunday brunch runs $6–9, and there's rooftop dining overlooking Courthouse Square.

Upscale

Aside from the Joshua-Wilton House, Harrisonburg's other establishment of note is the Amato family's **L'Italia Restaurant** (815 E. Market St., 540/433-0961, lunch and dinner daily), serving Italian fare amid candles and romantic music. Entrées such as lobster ravioli and the broiled catch of the day start at $10.

INFORMATION

Harrisonburg Tourism operates the local **visitors center** in the Hardesty Higgins House (212 S. Main St., 540/432-8935, www.harrisonburgtourism.com, 9 A.M.–5 P.M. daily).

NEAR HARRISONBURG
Farmers Markets

The flowing valley farmland surrounding Harrisonburg sets the stage for two examples of the original rural version of the shopping mall. Follow South Main Street out of town as it turns into U.S. 11 to reach the **Shenandoah Heritage Market** (540/433-3929, www.shenandoahmarket.com, 10 A.M.–6 P.M. Mon.–Fri., 9 A.M.–6 P.M. Sat.) on Route 11 south of I-81 exit 243, where you can browse Civil War memorabilia, antique tractors, model trains, crafts, and furniture as well as produce. A few miles further south on Route 42 between Bridgewater and Dayton is the **Dayton Farmers Market** (540/879-3801, www.daytonfarmersmarket.com, 9 A.M.–6 P.M. Thurs.–Sat.). Homemade breads, cheeses, and jellies fill dozens of booths next to country hams, jams, and toys.

Dayton

The centerpiece of the **Heritage Center** (Bowman and High Sts., 540/879-2681, www.heritagecenter.com, 10 A.M.–4 P.M. Mon.–Sat., $5) is a huge electric map that traces the comings, goings, and clashings of Stonewall Jackson's Shenandoah Valley Campaign. A 20-minute narrated tape explains things in dramatic tones. Regional ceramics, textiles, paintings, and sculptures fill the folk art section, close to a genealogy research library and bookstore.

Green Valley Book Fair

Some 40 years ago, Kathryn and Leighton Evans got the idea of selling surplus new and used books out of an old family barn. Today the idea has evolved into a huge affair filling three floors with half a million volumes on all subjects. New titles from most major publishers are 60–90 percent off retail—enough to entice buyers from nearby states. The Book Fair (2192 Green Valley Ln., 800/385-0099, www.gvbookfair.com) is held six times a year, for about two weeks at a time, March–December. It's in Mount Crawford off I-81 exit 240. Head east onto Route 682 for 1.5 miles, then take a left on Route 681 at the Green Valley sign. Contact them for a schedule.

Massanutten Resort

Some of the state's best skiing waits east of Harrisonburg in a natural depression behind Massanutten Peak. With the longest vertical drop in Virginia, Pennsylvania, or Maryland (1,100 ft.), Massanutten (540/289-9441, www.massresort.com) boasts 14 runs ranging from beginner to expert and six lifts, including Virginia's first quad. Other attractions include night skiing, a popular snowboard park, kids' programs, and NASTAR races. Lift tickets cost $45–64 adults, $40–54 children; tickets good for two hours at the state's first snow-tubing park are $18–22. (The latter often sell out the day before; call 800/207-6277 for availability.) Equipment rentals start at $24–34 per day for adults and $18–28 for children 12 and under. Look for late-season discounts on lift tickets in March.

During the rest of the year, Massanutten keeps busy with an 18-hole golf course, a water park, tennis courts, canoeing, kayaking, and a skate park. The chairlifts are open for scenic rides, and the mountain's trails are open for mountain bikes, but only to guests of the resort. Held on the opposite side of the mountain, the **Massanutten Hoo-Ha!** (540/289-4954) is an annual cross-country mountain bike race in June that's one of the largest in the state.

The resort is 10 miles from Route 33 on Route 644.

Natural Chimneys Regional Park

Seven limestone towers 65–120 feet tall form the nucleus of this small park near Mt. Solon (I-81 exit 240). The columns used to be part of the same block of limestone left from when Virginia was covered by an inland sea, but a layer of harder rock on top protected them from erosion. Natural Chimneys' other claim to fame is the **jousting tournaments** held the third Saturday of August to much medieval fanfare. Begun in 1821 to decide who should marry a local woman, they are among the oldest continually held sporting events in the country, older than the Kentucky Derby. No one crashes to the ground in full armor here, though—the tournaments are based on accuracy, with contestants aiming their lances through small rings at full gallop. The jousting tournament is now part of the Stone Tower Glenn Renaissance Faire (540/337-6324, www.medievalfantasiesco.com).

The park (540/245-5727, www.co.augusta.va.us, dawn–dusk daily, $2 pp or $5 per car) also has a campground (open May–Oct.) with 145 sites for $19–33 each, a pool, store, hot showers, and playground.

Grand Caverns Regional Park

Up there with Virginia's best, this network of caves includes huge Cathedral Hall, one of the largest underground rooms in the East, and the 5,000-square-foot Grand Ballroom, where dances were actually held in the early 1800s. This one was discovered in 1804 by a 17-year-old looking for a raccoon trap, making it the oldest show cave in the country, and was once visited by Thomas Jefferson on horseback from Monticello. Signatures on the walls record the quartering of Stonewall Jackson's troops near here during the Valley Campaign. More than 200 formations called "shields" are a mystery to geologists.

The caverns (540/249-5705, www.ci.grottoes.va.us, 9 A.M.–5 P.M. daily Apr.–Oct., weekends in Mar.–Nov. by appt., $18 adults, $11 children 6–12) are east of I-81 exit 235. Winter hours might be extended, beginning in November 2010; call to confirm. The park also encloses picnic shelters, hiking and biking trails, a pool, tennis courts, and a miniature golf course, and is host of a bluegrass festival the weekend after Labor Day.

Staunton and Vicinity

One of the oldest cities in the Shenandoah Valley, Staunton (pop. 24,000) is a pretty, if hilly, town to amble through for an afternoon or three. The Augusta County seat is home to yet another president and to country music luminaries the Statler Brothers, who opened for Johnny Cash for years.

Since it was spared from Civil War destruction, Staunton still claims historic architecture to rival that of any city in the state. Faded advertisements for feed, fertilizer, and hardware on brick buildings give the downtown a railroad-era look, while grand private homes fronted by sloping lawns line West Frederick Street. Intense restoration efforts have resurrected the train station and are now being focused on the warehouses of the adjacent Wharf area.

History

For a railroad town, Staunton (STAN-ton) is a surprisingly white-collar community, and has been for more than a century. Originally homesteaded by Scottish-Irish immigrant John Lewis in 1732, the town first served as a way station at the intersection of the old Valley Pike and the westbound Midland Trail, where travelers could rest themselves and their horses and stock up on supplies.

A little more than 50 years after the town was chartered, in 1801, the Central & Ohio Railroad arrived, beginning Staunton's transformation from a rural outpost to a thriving commercial city and transportation hub of western Virginia. Early on Staunton was on the map for doctors, lawyers, and educators looking for work, starting with the establishment of the Augusta County Courthouse (1745), the Western Lunatic Asylum (1825), and the Virginia School for the Deaf, Dumb, and Blind (1839). Those last two, thankfully, go by abridged names these days.

Woodrow Wilson was born here in 1856 to

Spared by Civil War shelling and modern-day demolition, Staunton has some of the best-preserved 19th-century architecture in the state.

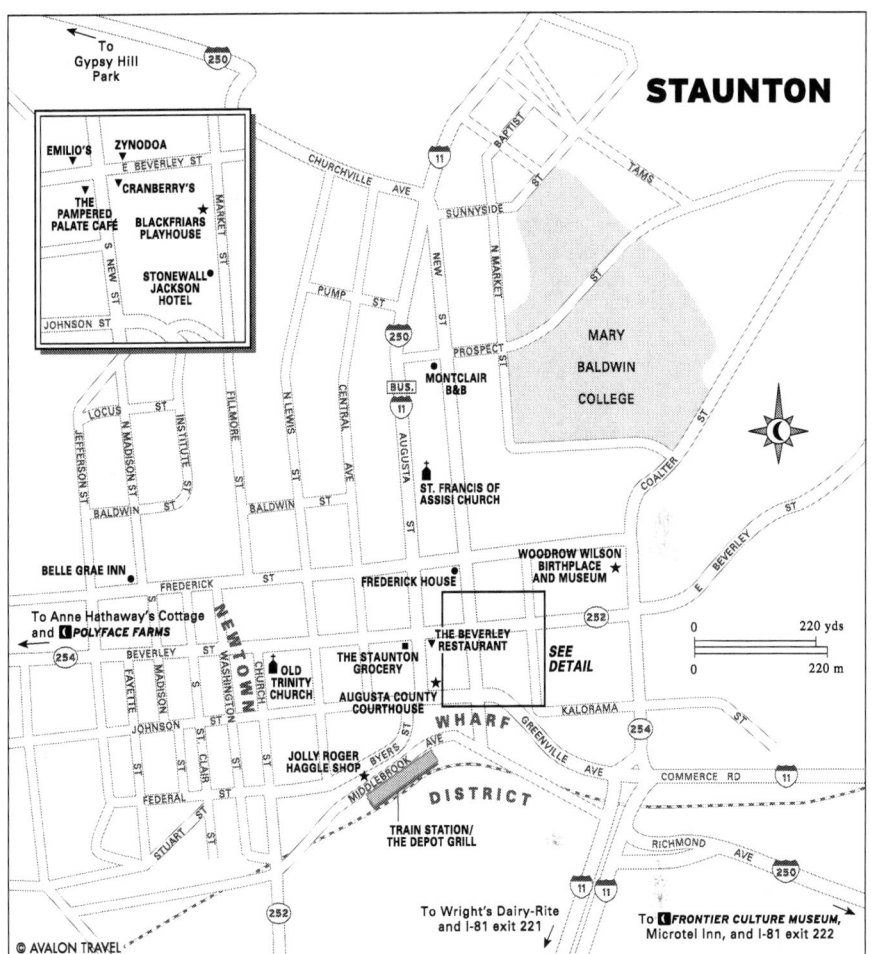

a local Presbyterian minister and his wife, and is immortalized in "Woody World" (the locals' nickname for the presidential library and museum). Staunton served as a supply base during the Civil War but was spared much of the destruction visited on other Virginia cities. That is why today Staunton boasts one of the best assemblages of 19th-century architecture in the state.

SIGHTS

No less than five lovingly preserved National Historic Districts earned Staunton a spot on the National Trust for Historic Preservation's 2001 list of a Dozen Distinctive Destinations nationwide. Historical-tour guide Marney Gibbs can give you the rundown aboard the Staunton Trolley (540/885-2403, www.stauntonguidedtours.com, $10 adults, $5 children) or one of her many walking or driving tours.

The cobble-lined **Wharf District** includes the early-1900s train depot (now an Amtrak station), with old cabooses at the end of a long platform that hummed with activity during the city's railroad heyday. Many of the nearby warehouses and mill buildings have been turned into galleries and antiques shops.

Beautiful Victorian buildings from the boom years of 1860–1920 fill the **Beverley** district, along the street of the same name between Lewis and Market Streets. West of Lewis Street is **Newtown,** actually the city's oldest residential area, home to prominent citizens and their less wealthy neighbors who labored in local factories. **Stuart Addition** adjoins the campus of Mary Baldwin College, and **Gospel Hill,** filled with elegant residences, gets it name from religious meetings originally held in the late 18th century.

◲ Frontier Culture Museum

In the 1700s, four ethnic groups—English, German, Scottish-Irish, and slaves from West Africa—dominated the small-scale farming settlements of the Shenandoah Valley frontier. Over the next two centuries, their distinctive traditions would blend into a uniquely American heritage brought back to life in this fascinating living-history center (540/332-7850, www.frontiermuseum.org, 9 A.M.–5 P.M. daily, 10 A.M.–4 P.M. daily Dec.–Mar., $10 adults, $6 children). With a focus on the common man rather than the patrician, the costumed interpreters and working farms set out to show how American immigrants lived, both in their home countries and here in the Virginia countryside. Ignore the traffic hum from I-81, and it's easy to be carried back in time by the smells of fresh-cut hay and open-hearth cooking and the sounds of cows lowing, pigs rooting, and the clank of hammer on anvil.

Start off at the visitors center, which offers films and a small museum explaining the Colonial cultures you're about to experience. Then step outside to begin a self-guided walking loop through six distinct farms. Rural life from the 18th and 19th centuries has been rigorously re-created and—with one notable exception—all the buildings are original: disassembled where they stood, shipped here, and reassembled on-site. Everything was done as authentically as possible, down to bringing in thatchers from Ulster to roof the Irish cottage.

The 18th-century **German farm** from the Rhineland-Palatinate region is first. A framework of thick posts and beams is covered with wattle and daub (woven sticks covered with a mixture of soil, water, sand, lime, and manure). This style became common in Colonial America, though wooden planks would eventually replace the twigs and fertilizer. Twin walls of whitewashed stone separated by a layer of rubble make up the early 19th-century **Scottish-Irish cottage** and outbuildings, one of which encloses a working forge. A small field is planted every spring with flax to make linen, a common crop in northern Ireland at the time. The 18th-century **English farmhouse** from West Sussex is the most substantial so far, a two-story wooden building with an elaborate brick chimney. Next comes along life in the New World, with a 1770s **clapboard-covered log house** from Rockingham County and an 1850s **homestead and tobacco barn** from Botetourt County near Roanoke.

Until recently, one culture was noticeably missing from the re-creations: the African. Recognizing this absence, the Frontier Museum's newest site, slated to open in fall 2010, is a **West African farmers compound** modeled after an Igbo village. Why the Igbo? Extensive research showed that nearly 40 percent of all African captives brought to Virginia during the Colonial era were Igbo, located in present-day Nigeria. With the help of Igbo building experts and scores of volunteers (among them local football players) the village is being hewn together mud brick by mud brick using traditional methods adapted to the Virginia soil. When complete, the village will include four houses, a perimeter wall, and a traditional garden including yams and livestock such as pygmy goats.

As the first of its kind in the United States, the village fills a unique cultural gap, allowing African Americans of Igbo descent to see their heritage up-close without having to fly to Nigeria, and encouraging all visitors to learn about West African contributions to common American life—even the small stuff, like quilt designs and fried okra. But most importantly, it shares what was until now a missing chapter in the story of the Virginia frontier.

The museum is on U.S. 250, west of I-81 exit 222. Most of the grounds and buildings are wheelchair-accessible, and motorized scooters are available free of charge to mobility-impaired visitors. A long list of daily demonstrations varies throughout the year, including fabric weaving, sheep shearing, woodworking, and cooking. Some of the more popular activities and events such as Oktoberfest and holiday lantern tours have special admission fees and require preregistration; call or check the website for details.

Woodrow Wilson Presidential Library & Museum

Only a few original presidential birthplaces are still open to the public (that cabin in Kentucky probably isn't the one where Lincoln was born), and this quaint city boasts one of them. The birthplace of the 28th president (18–24 N. Coalter St., 540/885-0897, www.woodrowwilson.org, 9 A.M.–5 P.M. Mon.–Sat., noon–5 P.M. Sun., reduced hours Nov.–Feb., $12 adults, $3 children 6–12) features period furniture; personal belongings; a collection of books, memoirs, and World War I volumes; and Wilson's favorite 1919 Pierce-Arrow limousine. Boxwood gardens outside were restored in 1993 by the Garden Club of Virginia. Guided tours and exhibits trace his life from here to Princeton and the White House. (Wilson only lived here for the first year of his life before moving to Georgia, but what the heck, it's a nice place.) Admission is free on his birthday, December 28.

Other Landmarks

The cream-brick **Augusta County Courthouse,** on the corner of Johnson and Augusta Streets, is the fifth such structure on this particular site. Its classic design includes large stone columns supporting a dome topped by a weather-greened statue of Justice. Dating to 1855, the Gothic Revival **Trinity Episcopal Church** on Beverley Street replaced one that hosted the Virginia General Assembly in 1787 (look for the 12 Tiffany stained-glass windows). The lime-green **St. Francis of Assisi Catholic Church** sits on the highest hill in town.

Mary Baldwin College (540/887-7019, www.mbc.edu) was founded by the Rev. Rufous Bailey in 1842 as the Augusta Female Seminary, making it one of the oldest women's colleges in the South. Today it has an enrollment of about 2,200 students. The Greek Revival campus buildings sit on 54 acres on Sycamore Street overlooking downtown. Tennis courts, playgrounds, a golf course, a skate park, and a swimming pool fill **Gypsy Hill Park,** northwest of downtown along Churchville Avenue.

ENTERTAINMENT AND RECREATION

Local artists are thankful for the **Staunton-Augusta Art Center** (20 S. New St., 540/885-2028, www.saartcenter.org), which holds opening receptions from time to time. Crafts such as paintings, pottery, jewelry, and scarves are sold near the holidays.

From late May to late October, free **guided walking tours** leave from the Woodrow Wilson Presidential Library & Museum at 10 A.M. every Saturday. Brochures are also available for self-guided rambles from the Staunton Visitors Center (35 S. New St., 540/332-3971, www.visitstaunton.com), or contact the Historic Staunton Foundation (540/885-7676, www.historicstaunton.org) for more information.

Gypsy Hill Park, at the intersection of Churchill and Thornrose Avenues, is a 214-acre expanse that includes a lake, a pool, a public golf course, a gymnasium, sports stadiums and fields, playgrounds, and a bandstand. The Gypsy Express miniature train still runs through the park as it has for 50 years (noon–6 P.M. Sat., 1–5 P.M. Sun., May–Oct., $1).

Pay a visit to Elizabethan England at the **Blackfriars Playhouse** (10 S. Market St., 540/851-1733 or 877/682-4236, www.americanshakespearecenter.com), home to the internationally acclaimed American Shakespeare Center. This 300-seat indoor

Staunton is best known for the Blackfriars Playhouse, but the Dixie is great for a movie.

playhouse—the only re-creation of the Bard's original indoor theater in the world—allows the productions to be staged as they originally were: on a simple stage sharing the same light as the audience section, giving a communal feel to the performances. The world-class venue is open year-round for Shakespeare productions and other special musical and theatrical events. Tours of the theater are also offered, often led by actors appearing in current productions (11 A.M. Mon.–Sat., plus 2 P.M. Mon.–Fri., $5).

Staunton also has two cool old-school cinemas. The **Dixie Theater** (125 E. Beverley St., 540/885-8445, www.thedixietheater.com, $6) has four screens and makes for a cheap date, and **Visulite Cinemas** (12 N. Augusta St., 540/885-9959, www.visulitecinemas.com, $8) has stadium seating with plush rocker-back chairs.

SHOPPING

Staunton's most interesting spot to browse is unquestionably the **Jolly Roger Haggle Shop** (27 Middlebrook Ave., 540/886-9527). Leave yourself an hour or more to do justice to roomfuls of old lunch boxes, turquoise jewelry, antique tools, militaria, books, and records piled to the ceiling. It boasts "more than one million items," and it's easy to believe. Other craft-antiques stores are clustered near Beverley and New Streets, including **Warehouse Antiques & Collectibles** (26 W. Beverley St., 540/885-0891), the city's largest antiques store, and **17 E. Beverley Antiques** (17 E. Beverley St., 540/885-1117, www.bevant.com), stocking vintage clothes, antique jewelry, quilts, and African art.

Sunspots (202 S. Lewis St., 540/885-0678) sells beautiful works in copper and handblown glass. You can watch the process during glass-blowing demos 10 A.M.–4 P.M. most days. The **Staunton/Augusta Farmers Market** (540/332-3802, www.safarmersmarket.com) features locally grown fruits, veggies, and other edibles on Saturday mornings April–November at Johnson and Byers Streets downtown.

EVENTS

The Stonewall Brigade Bandstand in Gypsy Hill Park is Staunton's music epicenter during the summer. The **Stonewall Brigade Band**, one of the nation's oldest continuous community bands, performs on Monday evenings June–August, and the **Jazz in the Park** series brings more music on Thursday evenings, rain or shine. In fact, you can basically pick a genre: There's also **gospel music** on Tuesday evenings and **bluegrass concerts** on Wednesdays. (All are free.) The **Staunton Music Festival** (540/569-0267, www.stauntonmusicfestival.com) offers classical and family music concerts at various locations around the city in August. Tickets are $20 per person.

ACCOMMODATIONS
$50-100
Near I-81 exit 222, the **Microtel Inn** (200 Frontier Dr., 540/887-0200) offers a heated outdoor pool, breakfast, and cookies at night.

$100-150
Fox-hunt decor distinguishes the **Montclair B&B** (320 N. New St., 540/885-8832 or 877 885-8832, www.montclairbnb.com). Sheri and Mark Bang have done an award-winning job of restoring the circa-1880 Italianate home, which features a library, private sitting rooms, and four guest rooms for $95-200.

The **Comfort Inn** (1032 Richmond Ave., 540/886-5000, $85-105) is between exit 222 off I-81 and downtown and offers free continental breakfast and an outdoor pool. There's also an **Econo Lodge** (1031 Richmond Ave., 540/885-5158, $60-130) in this price range near exit 222.

$150-200
The best way to top off a performance at Blackfriars Playhouse is a stay at **Anne Hathaway's Cottage** (950 W. Beverley St., 540/885-8885, www.anne-hathaways-cottage.com), a thatched-roof replica of Shakespeare's wife's cottage near Stratford in England. Rates for the three guestrooms are $160-210, including breakfast daily and afternoon tea on Friday and Saturday.

The most obvious place to stay in town is the restored **Stonewall Jackson Hotel** (24 S. Market St., 540/885-4848, www.stonewall

the historic Stonewall Jackson Hotel

jackson.com); you can't miss the rooftop neon sign. Built in 1924, the historic hotel has 124 rooms and suites ($100-200) that were renovated in 2005, an indoor pool, fitness center, and 24 Market, serving all meals daily. Theater packages are also available (Blackfriars is literally next door).

Over $200
Frederick House (28 N. New St., 540/885-4220 or 800/334-5575, www.frederickhouse.com) is a European-style inn with an attached tearoom across from Mary Baldwin College. (Enter from the parking lot on New Street.) The building, some parts of which date to 1810, features a Federal-style curving stairway. Twenty-three distinctive rooms and suites are spread between the main house and nearby cottages and townhouses. Prices range $103-273.

Up on the high western end of Frederick Street perches the **Belle Grae Inn** (515 W. Frederick St., 540/886-5151 or 888/541-5151, www.bellegrae.com). Originally part of a 200-acre

...n on the edge of town, the building known as the Old Inn was opened to the public in 1983. A front veranda and 12-foot ceilings grace the first of three Federal-style stories, and azaleas bloom in the garden in back. The circa-1873 Main Inn has three formal dining rooms and five rooms upstairs ($160–200). The Townhouse has two rooms and two suites ($160–220), and each of the four suites in the Jefferson House ($190) has a deck or porch overlooking the Victorian garden. The inn also serves up Thai specialties at the Ubon Thai Victorian Restaurant (540/886-4141, all meals daily).

Camping

In nearby Mint Springs off I-81 exit 217, the **Staunton Walnut Hills KOA** (484 Walnut Hills Rd., 540/337-3920 or 800/699-2568, www.walnuthillscampground.com) has a stocked fishing lake, pools, and laundry. The sites ($28–35) are open year-round, and cabins ($35–58) and cottages ($73–115) are available for rent as well.

FOOD
Snacks and Cafés

The **Pampered Palate Cafe** (28 E. Beverley St., 540/886-9463, lunch Mon.–Sat., dinner Fri.) offers quiches, pita sandwiches, and New York–style bagel sandwiches for $6–8. Many vegetarian and low-fat options are balanced by a gourmet goodie, coffee, and wine shop. Come by in the afternoon for "cappy hour" (i.e., cappuccino).

Staunton's oldest commercial building houses **Cranberry's** (7 S. New St., 540/885-4755), a natural grocery and eatery that serves excellent Lester's Best coffee and espresso, roasted daily by a local blues singer. Grab eggs and waffles for breakfast, or a smoothie and a BLT sandwich for lunch. Cranberry's also offers gluten-free items and has been certified by the Gluten-Free Restaurant Awareness Program. Open for breakfast and lunch Monday–Saturday, as well as dinner Thursday–Saturday, with shorter hours in winter.

Casual

Wright's Dairy-Rite (346 Greenville Ave., 540/886-0435, all meals daily) has been a local institution since 1952. Come inside or stay in your car for curbside service—either way, enjoy burgers, hot dogs, and sandwiches from $2 and up. The Statler Brothers, who hail from Staunton, used to fill up here.

Look for the stained-glass windows fronting the restored 1888 storefront of **The Beverley Restaurant** (12 E. Beverley St., 540/886-4317, all meals Mon.–Fri., breakfast and lunch only Sat.), serving home-style Southern food including chicken and dumplings, ham hocks and cabbage, and chipped-beef gravy breakfasts (all under $7). Both the chocolate milkshakes and the homemade pecan pies here are said to be "the best you'll ever eat" (let me know your verdict). They serve afternoon tea 3–5 P.M. Tuesday and Thursday.

Upscale

Today, more people head to the old C&O depot to try one of the two restaurants there than to board a train. **The Depot Grill** (42 Middlebrook Ave., 540/885-7332, lunch and dinner daily) boasts a marvelous 40-foot bar rescued from a luxury hotel that was demolished in Albany, New York. Seafood is also a favorite here, starting with shrimp, crab legs, and crawdads at the steamer bar. Sandwiches, burgers, and salads are $7–12, and entrées are $14–25.

Regional dishes like *pollo alla cacciatora* and gnocchi *alla bolognese* are a specialty of the cozy **Emilio's Italian Restaurant** (23 E. Beverley St., 540/885-0102, lunch and dinner daily). Casual lunches ($8–12) and dinners ($14–28) are enlivened by live music most nights in the upstairs Pompeii Lounge, boasting four fireplaces and a rooftop terrace that operate seasonally.

You won't mistake ◖ **The Staunton Grocery** (105 W. Beverley St., 540/886-6880, lunch Wed.–Sat., dinner Tues.–Sun.) for a supermarket; it's actually a fine-dining establishment renowned for chef Ian Boden's farm-to-table creations using fresh, local ingredients. Modern takes on Southern fare run $20–28 (appetizers are $7–11) in a stylishly casual setting with exposed brick walls and white tablecloths. Dishes follow the lines of roasted salmon with gnocchi, chestnuts, and brussels sprouts. Sundays are a three-course prix-fixe dinner for $35, and tasting menus paired with wine start at $55.

You know your culinary stars have aligned when the White House comes calling. Chef Michael Lund of **Zynodoa** (115 E. Beverley St., 540/885-7775, dinner daily, brunch at noon Sun.) cooks for the occasional presidential state dinner, but usually he's cooking up contemporary, locally sourced spins on fried green tomatoes and shrimp and grits here in Staunton. Start with cornmeal-dusted Chesapeake oysters (appetizers $9–12) before moving on to honey-brined pork tenderloin with apple sage bread pudding (entrées $18–27). One more vote of confidence: Lund trained at the Inn at Little Washington, widely considered the best in fine dining in Virginia.

INFORMATION

Look for the **Staunton/Augusta Travel Information Center** (1290 Richmond Rd., 540/332-3972 or 800/332-5219, 9 A.M.–5 P.M. daily) in the Museum of Frontier Culture, and the **Staunton Visitors Center** (35 S. New St., 540/332-3971, www.visitstaunton.com, 9 A.M.–6 P.M. daily, 9:30 A.M.–5:30 P.M. daily Nov.–Mar.) at the New Street Parking Garage. For information online, visit the city's website at www.staunton.va.us.

GETTING THERE AND AROUND

The free **Staunton Trolley** runs three different routes connecting downtown, the Wharf, and Gypsy Hill Park, among other destinations. There are designated stops, but you can also just flag them down. See the city website for hours and route details.

Trains leave the unstaffed **Amtrak** station for Charlottesville and Clifton Forge three times a week.

NEAR STAUNTON
Polyface Farms

Until recently, few living outside the Shenandoah Valley had heard of "beyond organic" farmer Joel Salatin and his 550-acre family-owned farm—no doubt because shipping farm-fresh meats runs counter to his commitment to buying and selling food locally. Then along came Michael Pollan's *New York Times* bestseller *The Omnivore's Dilemma* and the documentary *Food, Inc.,* and Salatin found himself standing front and center on the hay-bale soapbox of the sustainable agriculture movement.

Not that he had kept quiet before. The self-described Christian-Libertarian-Environmentalist-Capitalist-Lunatic has authored six books on raising pastured livestock and poultry using farming methods that focus on rotating animals' pastures daily to provide them with access to plentiful fresh air and grass (or, as he quips, "salad bars"). His goal is nothing short of changing the way we grow, buy, and sell food in America.

But don't just read about it here—see it for yourself. Polyface Farms (540/885-3590, www.polyfacefarms.com), so named for the "many faces," snouts, and beaks raised there, is deeply committed to the transparency of its operations and the treatment of its livestock. "Shake the hand that feeds you," the saying goes. Guided two-hour tours are available for $10.50 per person twice monthly (book early, they fill up).

Tour participants are invited to climb aboard a tractor-pulled flatbed of hay to visit the different pens and learn about farm operations and techniques. With Farmer Joel at the helm, it's kick-in-the-pants fun—really—and you'll see visitors there from all walks of life, from a retired couple from Ohio thinking about giving farming a go, to the usual suspects driving down from D.C. in an eco-friendly Prius. Kids especially will love the chick house, with all the downy yellow chicks milling about.

If you can't make it to one of the designated tours, visitors are still welcome to take a self-guided tour Monday–Saturday. Before you leave be sure to stock up on eggs, steaks, sausage, and chicken from the on-farm shop (9 A.M.–4 P.M. Sat. or by appointment). Polyface Farms is located in Swoope, about eight miles southwest of Staunton. Call or see website for directions.

Even if you never visit the farm, chances are good you'll eat a Polyface egg at some point during your time in Virginia. Once you start looking, you'll see "Polyface Farms" tattooed on restaurant menus from Washington, D.C., to Virginia Beach.

WAYNESBORO

Take exit 94 off I-81 to reach this industrial town just west of a major pass through the Blue Ridge. Accommodations await two blocks off Main Street at the **Belle Hearth B&B** (320 S. Wayne Ave., 540/943-1910 or 866/710-2256, www.bellehearth.com). Adorned with a gabled roof and wraparound porch, the early-1900s building is filled with Victorian furnishings and seven fireplaces—hence the name. Three rooms and one suite range $100–145.

The **P. Buckley Moss Museum** (150 P. Buckley Moss Dr., 800/343-8643, www.pbuckleymoss.com, 10 A.M.–5 P.M. Mon.–Sat., 12:30–5 P.M. Sun., free) houses dozens of works by the well-known local artist. Her distinctive "valley style," inspired by the scenery and people of the Shenandoah, is marked by bare, wiry trees, sensuous horses, chunky Canada geese, and elongated portraits of Amish and Old Order Mennonite farmers. There's a gift shop downstairs, where prices for even small prints can start in the hundreds.

Allegheny Highlands

Encompassing Highland, Bath, and parts of Augusta and Allegheny Counties, this wrinkled western spur is surprisingly accessible for such a wild area. Long, narrow peaks of the Allegheny Mountains ripple off into West Virginia, split by river valleys running arrow-straight southwest to northeast. With fewer than 3,000 people spread over 416 square miles, Highland County (aka Virginia's Switzerland) doesn't lack for open space. Most of it is above 4,000 feet elevation, making it one of the highest counties, in average elevation, east of the Mississippi. Many residents live off the land as their ancestors did, still referring to places as "three mountains over."

Bath County, in contrast, is one of the richest in Virginia, thanks to the fully realized resort possibilities of a series of thermal springs to which native tribes once ascribed healing powers. In 1750 a visiting doctor wrote, "the spring is very clear and warmer than new milk," although "the settlers would be better able to support travelers was it not for the great number of Indian warriors that frequently take what they want from them." Over the next few centuries, the wealthy residents of the Piedmont learned that the mountains and waters were the perfect escape from the summer mugginess. Thus began a tradition of lavish seasonal retreats, which is carried on today at the Homestead—possibly the grandest resort hotel in the state.

OUTDOOR RECREATION

Fishing is one of the top draws in this part of the state, attracting anglers from hundreds of miles away in search of bass (largemouth, smallmouth, and rock), trout, catfish, crappie, and muskies. Several of Virginia's major rivers have their headwaters in these choppy hills. Almost any of the streams and rivers flowing southwest, including the Maury, Bullpasture, and Cowpasture, offer great casting. The Jackson River flows into Lake Moomaw, a 12-mile flood-control reservoir with some of the best fishing in the state (bass in the three-to-four-pound range love the clear waters). The 60-acre Douthat Lake in Douthat State Park offers fee fishing for stocked trout.

Many wildlife management, recreation, and wilderness areas present boundless opportunities for hiking and camping amid the spruce and northern hardwood forests. Pocahontas County, just over the border in West Virginia, is a nationally known destination for mountain biking, and this side of the border is almost identical, although relatively less explored by knobby-tire enthusiasts. Finding your own track should be a cinch.

ACCESS

Possibly the prettiest road to the highlands—or anywhere in the state, for that matter—is Route 39, the "Avenue of Trees" from Lexington to Warm Springs via Goshen Pass. A 150-foot suspension bridge over the Maury River leads into tens of thousands of acres administered by the state. Frequent pull-offs and swimming spots galore can easily turn this 42-mile drive into a half-day trip. U.S. 250 from Staunton to Monterey comes in a close second, passing through the quaint burg of Churchville before becoming a rising corridor through the George Washington National Forest. A great view at the crest welcomes you to Highland County before the road inches its tortuous way down the other side of the ridge, only to rise and fall, again and again. Finally, no-nonsense I-64 heads from Lexington straight into West Virginia.

There's an unstaffed **Amtrak** station (307 E. Ridgeway St., 800/872-7245) in Clifton Forge, with trains to Staunton and White Sulphur Springs, West Virginia, and through bus service to Roanoke.

MONTEREY

Coming over the mountain on U.S. 250 when the leaves are lush and green can make the Highland County seat seem like a vision, nestled as it is in a narrow, gently sloping valley. It's a small town, with about 200 people at last count and only one traffic light (a flashing one, at that). U.S. 250 turns into Main Street as it runs through the center of town, lined with dozens of old buildings from the turn of the 20th century or before. The Landmark House, across from the courthouse, was built from logs in 1790 and renovated in 1977.

Recreation

For guiding and instruction in rock climbing, contact Rick Lambert at **Highland Adventures** (540/468-2722). Cyclists will be keen to explore the country roads; download maps and cue sheets of suggested routes from the Highland County Chamber of Commerce website (www.highlandcounty.org). In August, the **Mountain Mama Road Bike Challenge** (540/468-2946, www.bikemountainmama.homestead.com) stages a century ride with nearly 14,000 feet of climbing that quickly introduces you to the terrain and the vistas (there are shorter rides too).

Shopping

Opposite the courthouse sits the **H&H Cash Store** (540/468-2570, www.handh.homestead.com), an old-fashioned mercantile stocking maple sugar candy, buckwheat flour, tools, and clothing. As they say, "If we don't have it, you don't need it." Knitters and crocheters can pick up specialty yarns, many of them locally made, at **Wool Becomes Ewe** (50 Fleisher Ave., 540/468-2007, www.woolbecomesewe.com), a block north of Main Street. Highland County is typically one of Virginia's largest wool-producing counties, so you can thank the sheep you'll see grazing on the hillsides later. The **Highlands Farmers Market** runs Friday afternoons June through September at the Highland Center (540/468-1922), located south on Spruce Street just off U.S. 250.

Events

Fans of Virginia fairs know Monterey's **Highland Maple Festival** is one of the first major ones of the year. Held the second and third weekends in March, the festival centers on the fact that Highland is the only county in Virginia that produces maple syrup and all its tasty by-products. Some 50,000 people eager to see the sun after a long winter make the trek to enjoy crafts and an all-you-can-eat pancake breakfast—topped with fresh maple syrup, of course.

Accommodations

The pink stone **Montvallee Motel** (54 E. Main St., 540/468-2500, www.montvalleemotel.com) offers 1950s style charm at the intersection of U.S. 250 and U.S. 220, with double rooms for $84–120. Farther on into town sits the Victorian **Highland Inn** (68 W. Main St., 540/468-2143 or 888/466-4682, www.highland-inn.com, $100–150), built in 1904 as a vacation getaway. Gingerbread trim decorates the stacked front porches, where rocking chairs sway in the breeze. Inside are the Black Sheep Tavern and a dining room, both heated by wood-burning stoves for cooler evenings.

The **Cherry Hill Bed & Breakfast** (224 W. Mill Alley, 540/468-1900 or 540/468-2020, www.cherryhillbandb.com, $85–110) perches on Mill Alley one block off Main Street. Bay windows look out over a wraparound porch to a great view of the town and valley, and a hammock sways in the quiet flower garden out back.

Contact the Highland County Chamber of Commerce (540/468-2550, www.highlandcounty.org) for information on the many other cabins, farms, and other rural getaways in the area.

Food

The **Monterey Dining Room** of the Highland Inn serves dinner Wednesday–Saturday and a brunch buffet on Sunday. Caesar salads and burgers are $8–9 and entrées such as locally caught rainbow trout and pecan-crusted chicken are $14–18, with nightly specials for a bit more.

Across the street, **High's Restaurant** (73 W. Main St., 540/468-1700, all meals daily) is the oldest in town and still going strong. You'll usually find it bustling with local folks. Burgers and sandwiches cost $4–6 while T-bones and trout can cost up to $20. The homemade pies and fresh bread are worth a stop. Cash only.

Information

The **Highland County Chamber of Commerce** (540/468-2550, www.highlandcounty.org) has an office in the Highland Center on Spruce Street.

Near Monterey

A wealth of hiking options await in **Laurel Fork,** a 10,000-acre special management area that covers the tip of the point sticking into West Virginia. This pristine region shelters "relic communities" left over from cooler times, including rare species such as the endangered Virginia northern flying squirrels, which soar through the red spruce forests.

Dozens of miles of trails roam through the craggy hills, many following old railroad grades. Popular ones include the Buck Run and Locust Springs Run Trails, following turn-of-the-20th-century railroad grades once used to log virgin timber. You can make an 11-mile loop (actually a figure eight) out of the Buck Run, Spring Run, Cold Spring, and Christian Run Trails, starting at the Locust Spring Picnic Area. (Be ready for a number of stream crossings.)

See the Highland County Chamber of Commerce website (www.highlandcounty.org) for directions to the trailhead, which involves a number of twists and turns on gravel roads. Contact the Warm Springs Ranger District of the George Washington & Jefferson National Forest (540/839-2521, www.fs.fed.us/r8/gwj/warmsprings) for more information.

If Monterey isn't far enough away for you, consider staying at the **Bear Mountain Farm and Wilderness Retreat** (540/468-2700, www.mountain-retreat.com, open Apr.–Oct.), a lodge so far into the hinterlands that you could throw a rock and hit West Virginia. The center welcomes everyone from individuals to groups of up to 20, who can stay in three simple, snug pine cabins with shared bathhouse ($90–125) or the larger Allegheny Mountain log cabin ($125), which sleeps five and feels straight out of the Wyoming foothills. The latter has a large common room with a piano, cooking facilities, a hot tub, and spectacular views from the wide windows and wraparound porch. The owners offer naturalist weekend workshops and guided hikes. Relax in the evening in front of the wood-burning stove in the main room or in the sand-floored sauna. Camping is $35, or $45 with use of the kitchen and bathhouse. The stargazing, as you can imagine, is divine, but be sure to arrive at Bear Mountain before dark to avoid getting lost.

Some of the most isolated and craggy territory in the George Washington National Forest fills the 6,500-acre **Ramsey's Draft Wilderness,** which you enter off U.S. 250 about 21 miles east of Monterey. Thousands of acres of virgin forest—spared the axe thanks to their inaccessibility—include yellow poplar, white oaks, and hemlocks, making up one of the largest expanses of old-growth forest in the East. ("Draft" means creek, and you'll cross plenty while hiking here.) The 6.8-mile Ramsey's Draft Trail winds alongside a stream of the same name, and a National Forest campground sits nine miles north of U.S. 250 on Route 715 (continue one mile northeast on Forest Road 95, then one mile southwest on Forest Road 95B). Call the North River Ranger District of the George Washington & Jefferson National Forests in Staunton (540/885-8028, www.fs.fed.us/r8/gwj/northriver) for more information.

WARM SPRINGS

The Bath County seat nestles in a valley near a small set of natural thermal springs. Eighteenth-century buildings, many white with green trim, constitute the original town center known as Old Germantown off Route 39 just west of U.S. 220.

Recreation

A pair of oddly shaped buildings at the Route 39/U.S. 220 intersection house the **Jefferson Pools,** owned by the luxury resort The Homestead. These large stone pools of naturally warm water were built in the late 18th century, when the Virginia elite would make the rounds of different pools in the area. Thomas Jefferson may have lent his design flair to the structures: the men's pool house has 8 sides and the women's has 22. Jefferson spent three weeks here in 1818, soaking three times a day and deeming the spring waters "of first merit."

As you relax in the 98°F water, be thankful fashions have changed since the 1830s, when according to one account stylish bathers had to don "a large cotton gown of a cashmere shawl pattern lined with crimson, a fancy Greek cap, Turkish slippers, and a pair of loose pantaloons." For a change of pace, try hydrotherapy, where part of the 1,200-gallon-per-minute flow is released onto your back as you sit in a special chamber outside and below the pool. The clothing-optional pools are open noon–5 P.M. seasonally for $17 per hour. Call the Homestead concierge to confirm hours (540/839-7741).

Accommodations and Food

Take Old Germantown Road (Rte. 692) off Route 39 toward the center of Warm Springs to reach the **Anderson Cottage Bed & Breakfast** (540/839-2975, www.bbonline.com/va/anderson) on your left. The two buildings are among Bath County's oldest, having served over the years as a tavern, a girls' school, and a summer inn. They've been in the present owner's family since the 1870s. Rates range $100–150; the separate guest cottage, formerly an early-19th-century brick kitchen, is $150 for the first night and $125 per night thereafter.

To find **The Inn at Gristmill Square** (540/839-2231, www.gristmillsquare.com), look for the waterwheel on Old Mill Road (Rte. 645) in the heart of Warm Springs. A mill has stood here since 1771, but the present buildings date to the 19th century. Janice and Jack McWilliams, who bought the place in 1981, have added tennis courts, a pool, and a sauna in the process of restoring five buildings: the Blacksmith Shop, the Miller House, the Steel House, and the Hardware Store. All 17 guest rooms have wood-burning fireplaces and are tastefully furnished with antiques and exotic curios. Rates ($110–175) include a continental breakfast. Fine food is served with a country flair in the adjacent **Waterwheel Restaurant.** Dinner, served daily, features savory dishes such as roast duck with apricots ($24–30). Sunday brunch is also available.

Three **National Forest campgrounds** can be found within 20 miles of Warm Springs, all starting west on Route 39. From nearest to farthest, they are Hidden Valley ($10), Blowing Springs ($10), and Bolar Mountain

($16–20) on Lake Moomaw. Blowing Springs is open year-round; the other two just April–November. Contact the George Washington & Jefferson National Forest (540/839-2521, www.fs.fed.us/r8/gwj/warmsprings) for exact directions and more information.

ON THE ROAD TO HOT SPRINGS

Virginia novelist Mary Johnson *(To Have and to Hold)* built the central part of **Three Hills Inn & Cottages** (540/839-5381 or 888/234-4557) in 1913. Today the hotel, which is reached by a winding driveway from U.S. 220, commands an impressive view from 38 acres of hillside just south of the Route 39/U.S. 220 intersection. Rooms in the main house are $130–150, suites are $180–270, and several cottages with kitchenettes can hold four people for $300. Some rates include a full breakfast.

This neck of the woods also happens to be home to one of Virginia's most celebrated musical venues, the not-for-profit **Garth Newel Music Center** (540/839-5018 or 877/558-1689, www.garthnewel.org). Top-flight classical performances are held in the concert hall on Saturday and Sunday afternoons. You can enjoy a four- or five-course set meal (reservations required) or picnic before or after the shows. In mid-June, the music center hosts the **Virginia Blues & Jazz Festival,** which has featured renowned musicians like Taj Mahal. Contact the center for prices and a current schedule.

HOT SPRINGS
◖ The Homestead

Virginia's premier resort (540/839-1766 or 866/354-4653, www.thehomestead.com) is more like a richly endowed university than a hotel. So big that U.S. 220 curves around it and little arrows are posted to help navigate the hallways, this world-class spread covers 15,000 acres of Bath County with spotless grounds, stately brick buildings, and one of the finest mountain golf courses in the country.

The first lodge here was built in 1766 by Lt. Thomas Bullitt, a frontier militiaman. The facilities were improved to the status of "modern hotel" in the mid-19th century, just in time to serve as a field hospital during the Civil War. The first spa, golf course, and tennis courts were opened in 1892, but most of the buildings vanished in a fire in 1901 and were rebuilt.

Inside the main structure, the cavernous Great Hall is lined with fireplaces surrounded by cozy chairs. The opulent President's Lounge has a view of the inner courtyard, and the Jefferson Parlor features wall paintings of Thomas Jefferson and the Homestead. For meals, guests can choose between the formal main dining room, 1766 Grille, and several more casual options, such as the Casino Club or Sam Snead's Tavern. Cottage Row off the Great Hall contains a small mall's worth of shops selling fine gifts, children's items, and gourmet foods. Golf, ski, and tennis shops elsewhere in the complex rent and sell sporting goods.

The Homestead offers more than enough activities to keep guests busy year-round, both indoors and out. Three golf courses—including the regular top-100 contender Cascades Course, restored to its original 1923 William Flynn design—draw the most visitors. One boasts the oldest first tee in the country, in use since 1890. Instruction and full equipment services are available for golfers and patrons of the hotel's six tennis courts. Canoeing, mountain biking, and 100 miles of hiking trails lure hikers into the hills, and there's a four-mile private trout stream and a shooting club for the sporting types. Guests can take lessons in both fly fishing and falconry.

One of the first European-style spas in the country offers aromatherapy, hydrotherapy, massage therapy, facials, and an indoor spring-fed pool opened in 1903. Bowling alleys and a movie theater keep night owls busy, and the Homestead Kids' Club keeps children occupied. In the winter, a small **ski area**—the South's first—has nine slopes, a snowboard park, snow-making equipment, and a full-service ski shop. If you're not a downhill speed demon, snowshoe and snowmobile tours and cross-country ski lessons are also available.

The hotel has 480 rooms and suites. Standard room rates range $175–315 per night on summer weekends. Suites can cost as much as triple that rate. Various golf, spa, and romance packages are also available.

DOUTHAT STATE PARK

Virginia's oldest state park (540/862-8100, www.dcr.virginia.gov/state_parks/dou.shtml, $2 per car, $3 weekends) is also one of its best. It boasts 40 miles of hiking and mountain biking trails winding through 4,493 rugged acres, blustery ridges, and deep forest surrounding 50-acre Douthat Lake, stocked twice a week with rainbow trout (as is Wilson Creek below the dam). Three miles of the creek have been designated children-only, giving budding anglers easy access and clearings to perfect their casts into well-stocked pools. Douthat is the only Virginia state park split by a road—Route 629, which leaves I-64 north from exit 27.

Campsites (open Mar.–Nov.) are $24–25 each, and reservations are essential on busy weekends from Memorial Day to Labor Day. One-room, one-bedroom, and two-bedroom cabins are priced $88–112 (less on weekdays and off-season). Two five-bedroom lodges can be rented by the week or for a minimum of two nights: The **Creasey Lodge** is $270–301 per night for up to 18 people, and the **Main Lodge** is $318–354 per night for up to 15 (both are also cheaper on weekdays and off-season). Three new cabins were under construction in 2010. Swimming from the beach area is $2–3 per person. A restaurant overlooking the lake serves lunch and dinner Wednesday–Friday and all meals on weekends from Memorial Day to Labor Day, and weekends in April and October. There's also a camp store and gift shop.

Lexington

Take a smallish mannerly town, steep it in Civil War history, overlay with a nationally recognized college or two, and you'll end up with something approaching this quiet community (pop. 7,000), close to both Natural Bridge and the Blue Ridge Parkway. Crew-cut cadets stroll in gray full dress uniform down tree-shaded streets, while other students jog in red and yellow school colors past grand colonnaded houses. Within the town limits lie two of the most honored heroes of the Confederacy: Robert E. Lee and Stonewall Jackson.

Founded in 1777, Lexington was leveled by fire in 1796 and rebuilt with lottery proceeds. Less than 30 years after its founding, the Virginia Military Institute (VMI) had a chance to prove its mettle, when dozens of cadets were thrown into the Battle of New Market in May 1864. VMI was the target of Union Gen. David Hunter's guns a month later. The barracks and much of town were left in ruins.

Since then, things have improved. In 2000 the city was included in the National Trust for Historic Preservation's list of a Dozen Distinctive Destinations, representing some of the best-preserved and unique communities in America.

SIGHTS
Washington and Lee University

Known as "W and L," this small private college (540/458-8400, www.wlu.edu) enjoys a national reputation, with an overwhelming percentage of students arriving from the top of their high school classes. It was founded in 1749 and saved from bankruptcy in 1796 by a substantial gift from George Washington. Soon after conceding the Civil War at Appomattox, Robert E. Lee served as its president from 1865 to 1870. Today, 2,000 students enjoy a beautiful central campus that was declared a National Historic Landmark in 1972. A row of dark redbrick buildings are fronted by bright white colonnades.

In the center of the campus stands the **Lee Chapel and Museum** (540/458-8768, http://chapelapps.wlu.edu, 9 A.M.–5 P.M. Mon.–Sat., 1–5 P.M. Sun. Apr.–Oct., to 4 P.M. Nov.–Mar.,

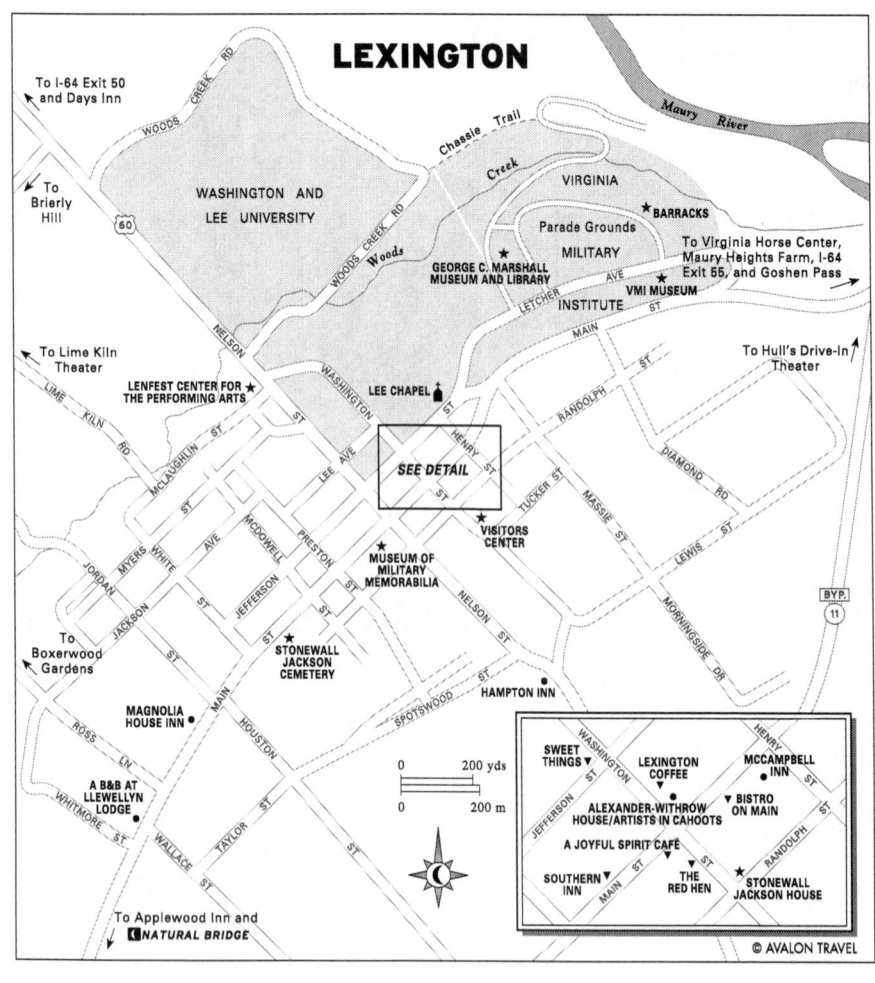

free). The former Confederate commander supervised its construction in 1867–1868 and set up his offices in the lower level. The simple, pretty Romanesque chapel (not to be confused with the Robert E. Lee Episcopal Church, at Washington St. and Lee Ave.) was actually never consecrated, serving instead as a hall for meetings and weddings. Inside is Charles Wilson Peale's portrait of George Washington—the first Washington ever sat for—in the incongruous uniform of a British colonel. A famous Edward Valentine statue of Lee in repose is surrounded by Confederate flags. Notice that Lee is represented not as dead, but resting: His feet are crossed and his hand rests on the hilt of his sword. Downstairs are the Lee family crypt and a small museum, which includes Lee's office just as he left it on September 28, 1870. Lee's horse Traveler is buried outside.

Virginia Military Institute

The country's first state military college

(540/464-7211, www.vmi.edu), VMI was founded in 1839 on the site of the Lexington Arsenal and had an initial class of 23. Twenty-five years later, 1864 was a big year for VMI: in May, her cadets fought in the Battle of New Market, and in June the barracks were shelled to the ground by Federal forces. The next big news came more than a century later. In 1996, the U.S. Supreme Court ruled that the school's males-only policy was unconstitutional, and a year later 30 female cadets were allowed to endure the infamous freshman Rat Line, a harsh rite of passage that claims 25 percent of each incoming class. The "cadettes" lived on the same floors as the men, wearing the same crew cuts, under the rule that any fooling around will result in the dismissal of both parties. New outdoor security lighting, emergency phones, and modified communal bathrooms made the adjustment slightly easier. In 2001, the institute's first coed class graduated without any major incidents to mar the transition.

Crenellations (battlements) top somber gray buildings around the huge central parade ground where cadets practice sports and military drills. (The Corps of Cadets gives a review parade most Friday afternoons.) At the southwest corner, the **George C. Marshall Museum and Library** (540/463-7103, www.marshall foundation.org, 9 A.M.–5 P.M. Tues.–Sat., 1–5 P.M. Sun., $5 adults, $2 students) commemorates the 1901 graduate who went on to serve as general of the army, the highest military rank possible. While he was secretary of state, his Marshall Peace Plan for the rebuilding of Europe after World War II won him the Nobel Peace Prize. The museum contains army memorabilia, personal papers, and a narrated map of World War II.

The **Virginia Military Institute Museum** (540/464-7334, www.vmi.edu/museum, 9 A.M.–5 P.M. daily, free) is located in Jackson Memorial Hall at the opposite corner of the parade ground. Stonewall Jackson's field desk and a statue of his favorite horse, Little Sorrel, are both on display along with period clothes, weapons, and historical VMI artifacts. The museum reopened in 2006 following a two-year $3.3 million expansion.

Stonewall Jackson House

The only home the Confederate commander ever owned stands in the heart of Lexington (8 E. Washington St., 540/463-2552, www .stonewalljackson.org, 9 A.M.–5 P.M. Mon.–Sat., 1–5 P.M. Sun., Mar.–Dec., $6 adults, $3 children 6–17). Jackson occupied the modest brick townhouse for two years with his second wife, Anna Morrison, before riding off to war in April 1861, never to return. Restored in 1979, the brick building contains many of his possessions and other Civil War–era pieces, along with a gift shop. The kitchen garden has been replanted behind the house. Tours are given every half-hour until 4:30 P.M.

Stonewall Jackson Cemetery

After being accidentally shot by his own men at Chancellorsville, "Old Jack" was finally laid to rest in this burial ground at the south end of Main Street. An Edward Valentine statue

Stonewall Jackson Cemetery

STONEWALL JACKSON

Born Thomas Jonathan Jackson on January 21, 1824, in Clarksburg, Virginia, the Civil War's most famous field commander found himself an orphan by age seven. He grew up in the house of an uncle, before squeaking into the U.S. Military Academy at West Point. (The first choice from the local congressional district, it seemed, had quit after his first day.) There he survived, in his own words, "by the skin of my teeth," graduating in 1846, 17th in a class of 59.

During the Mexican-American War, Jackson saw action in Cerro Gordo, Veracruz, and Chapultepec, and his outstanding conduct in the artillery earned him early promotions. In 1851, though, he left the rank of major to become a professor of military tactics and physics at the Virginia Military Institute (VMI). Students derided his dull teaching style and classroom quirks, starting with a shrill voice that belied his six-foot, 170-pound frame. Jackson lived in Lexington for the next decade, joining the Presbyterian Church and local Bible society. Two of those years were spent in the house on Washington Street, which is now a museum.

Within weeks of the outbreak of the Civil War, Jackson was back in the ranks, assuming a post as infantry colonel on April 21, 1861. Quickly promoted to brigadier general, the former teacher marched a group of VMI cadets to Richmond to help train the budding Confederate Army. His famous nickname came at the First Battle of Bull Run, in July 1861, soon after Confederate forces had begun to flee the fight. Seeing Jackson's troops holding their ground, Brig. Gen. Barnard E. Bee cried, "There stands Jackson like a stone wall! Rally behind the Virginians!" Bee was killed minutes later, but the tide of battle turned, and the name stuck.

Shortly after being promoted to major general, Stonewall cemented his place in history with his famous Valley Campaign in the spring of 1862, often called one of the most brilliant in military history. He continued to shine through the battles of Antietam and Second Bull Run, where his unorthodox tactics and uncanny rapport with General Lee won him fight after fight. Stonewall worked best when he was free to march and attack at will, pushing his men to the limit and always appearing when and where his opponents least expected.

Through it all, "Old Jack" remained a strange bird, obsessed with secrecy and concealing his plans even from direct subordinates. (Maj. Gen. Richard Ewell eventually concluded that his superior was a few pecks short of a bushel.)

At Chancellorsville in early May 1863, Jackson detached from General Lee's forces to flank the Federal XI Corps under Maj. Gen. Joseph Hooker. The risky but inspired maneuver routed the enemy troops in one of the most dramatic and decisive Confederate victories of the war. But Stonewall's finest hour was too soon followed by his final one: Out riding the evening of May 2, he was fired on by mistake by Confederate soldiers. Two of his aides were killed, and Jackson was shot in the right hand and left arm. In a nearby home that served as a field hospital, doctors decided to amputate the shattered limb. "He has lost his left arm," Lee said as Jackson lay dying, "but I have lost my right."

Jackson gave a good fight, but pneumonia set in and his condition deteriorated. On May 10, his doctors decided that he wouldn't last until sundown. The Confederacy's star commander died that afternoon after a final request: "Let us cross over the river and rest in the shade of the trees." His valiant Stonewall Brigade, hardened by dozens of battles, was never the same after losing its leader, though eight of its men went on to become generals.

WIKIMEDIA COMMONS

The fabled general and 144 Confederate veterans are buried in Lexington's Stonewall Jackson Cemetery.

marks his tomb in the center, surrounded by the graves of other Civil War notables and prominent local citizens. Open dawn–dusk.

Boxerwood Gardens

Local doctor Robert Munger began planting rare trees and shrubs around his house in 1952. After his death in 1988, his gardener bought the place and opened it to the public in 1997. More an arboretum than a flower garden, Boxerwood (963 Ross Rd., 540/463-2697, www.boxerwood.org, dawn–dusk daily, free) encloses 15 bucolic acres of exotic species such as Japanese maples and dwarf conifers alongside local dogwoods, rhododendrons, and azaleas, all with a panoramic view of the Blue Ridge Mountains. Everything is labeled, but the atmosphere is more raggedly natural than neatly pruned. Maps are available for self-guided tours, but half the fun is simply wandering around and seeing what you find.

Museum of Military Memorabilia

Uniforms, weapons, flags, and accoutrements from France, Great Britain, Germany, and the United States fill this small gallery (122 S. Main St., 540/464-3041, noon–5 P.M. Wed.–Fri., 9 A.M.–5 P.M. Sat., Apr.–Oct., $3 adults). The collection spans wars from 1740 to the Gulf War, and guided tours are available. Cadets in uniform are admitted free.

Virginia Horse Center

On Route 39 just north of I-64 lies one of the most outstanding equine complexes in the country. The 600-acre state-of-the-art center (540/464-2950, www.horsecenter.org) hosts shows, clinics, and sales year-round, including the Spring Arabian Classic, the Virginia Horse Trials, and the Southern States Showdown. The **American Work Horse Museum** includes just about everything horse-powered you can think of, from farm equipment to rural postal wagons. It's open most weekends or whenever an equine event takes place.

ENTERTAINMENT AND RECREATION

Theaters

On the outskirts of Lexington, the ruins

of a 19th-century kiln have been converted into one of the more unusual and enjoyable places to see a play in the entire mid-Atlantic region. Founded in 1983, the **Lime Kiln Theater** (540/463-7088, www.theateratlimekiln.com) seems to rise up out of the ground, amid the vine-covered stones where workers once smelted lime and cut stones. Actors and musicians now perform on summer evenings on one of three stages—two open to the stars and one in a tent in case of rain. The outdoor theater season runs April–October. Tickets for plays and concerts are $8–55 and are available for purchase by calling 540/463-7088 or at the Lexington Visitors Center. Reach the theater from Lime Kiln Road off White and McLaughlin from Main Street, or via Border Road south off U.S. 60 West.

Washington and Lee's **Lenfest Center for the Performing Arts** (U.S. 60 West and Glasgow St., 540/458-8000, http://lenfest.wlu.edu) also hosts plays and concerts by students and professionals. The W&L Film Society also screens movies at the **University Commons** at the corner of Main and Henry Streets, often free. Head north on Route 11 about five miles to reach the classic dinosaur called **Hull's Drive-in Theater** (540/463-2621, www.hullsdrivein.com, $6 pp over age 12), one of only a handful of drive-in theaters left in the state. It's the real thing, Sno-Cones and all. Open since 1950, it's been operated by a nonprofit group called Hull's Angels since 2001, making it the country's only nonprofit, community-owned drive-in theater.

Nightlife

Students name **The Palms** (101 W. Nelson St., 540/463-7911) as the biggest and most popular bar in town. It's open from lunch (sandwiches and burgers) through dinner (light fare to chicken and pasta) until 1 or 2 A.M.

Tours

Lexington is one of the most pleasant towns in Virginia to wander around on foot. Pick up a self-guided **walking-tour brochure** from the visitors center, detailing four different routes.

From late May to October, **Haunting Tales of Historic Lexington** (540/464-2250) guarantees a scare—or at least a shiver—on candlelit rounds of ghostly sites around town. The 90-minute walking tour leaves at 8:30 P.M. from the visitors center, where tickets ($12 adults, $6 children 4–12) are available. Reservations are required; cash only.

A daytime option is a tour of Lexington's major historical sights by horse-drawn carriage with the **Lexington Carriage Company** (540/463-5647, www.lexcarriage.com). Its 45-minute tours leave from Washington Street across from the visitors center, 11 A.M.–5 P.M. daily April–October, 10 A.M.–6 P.M. daily June–August, $16 adults, $7 children 7–13.

The folks at the Applewood Inn (242 Tarn Beck Ln., 540/463-1962 or 800/463-1902, www.applewoodbb.com) organize two-hour **llama treks** into the surrounding countryside for $24 per person ($18 for guests of the inn).

Outdoor Recreation

Narrow but pretty **Woods Creek Park** follows the creek of the same name for two miles along the length of Lexington. At the northern end, where it reaches the Maury River, you can pick up the **Chessie Nature Trail,** a seven-mile stretch of the old Chesapeake and Ohio rail line through rural countryside to Buena Vista. Damage from Hurricane Camille in 1969 caused the line to be abandoned, allowing the Nature Conservancy to acquire it in 1978. Along the way you'll pass old canal locks and cross a 235-foot bridge over the South River near its confluence with the Maury River. To reach the starting point, cross U.S. 11 near VMI Island using the foot bridge; the pedestrian trail begins near the north end of the U.S. 11 bridge.

Fly-fishing guide extraordinaire **John Roberts** (540/463-3235 or 800/882-1145, www.vatrout.com) will take you casting in trout-rich local streams for $350–490 per day and offers casting instruction for $30 per hour. Prices include all equipment except waders, which he rents.

Afternoon canoeing, kayaking, and tubing trips on the Maury and James Rivers can

THE DEVIL'S MARBLEYARD

A short but challenging hike up the west side of the Blue Ridge leads to a singular hillside strewn with white quartzite boulders. Split by frost wedges during the last Ice Age, these rocks cover eight acres, leading to a great view of Arnold's Valley from the top. (Watch for spiders and biting insects in the summer, though.) To get there, take Route 130 south from Natural Bridge to Natural Bridge Station, then take a right on Route 759 (Arnold's Valley Rd.). Cross the James River and the Shenandoah Valley, pass a correctional center on the left, then head left on Petite's Gap Road at a three-way intersection. Parking is on the left, marked Belfast Trail. The trail is only a mile long but strewn with stones, and a few creek crossings are necessary. You can access the Appalachian Trail from the top, and it's easiest to descend on the trail to the right of the rockslide.

You'll find a little bit of everything—and then some—at **Goodharts Second Hand Shop** (7 S. Jefferson St., 540/463-7559), from crates of records and old guitars to photographs, clothes, and antiques. For books, head to Nelson Street: Try **The Bookery** (107 W. Nelson St., 540/464-3377) or **Books & Co.** (29 W. Nelson St., 540/463-4647), which also sells CDs and maps.

Lexington has too many antiques stores to mention—practically one on every block—but for sheer volume you can't beat the **Lexington Antique Center** (1495 N. Lee Hwy., 540/463-9511), with 250 dealers spread over 20,000 square feet. It's in the College Square Shopping Center, north off Lee-Jackson Highway, near both I-81 exit 191 and I-64 exit 55.

EVENTS

Lee-Jackson Day commemorates the birthdays of Robert E. Lee (January 19) and Stonewall Jackson (January 21) with celebrations throughout the South, but particularly in Stonewall's hometown. Free tours of Jackson's home and other festivities honor the local hero.

In March of election years, Lexington comes alive with Washington and Lee's famous **Mock Convention** (http://mockcon.wlu.edu), an outrageous parade and party that also happens to be one of the most accurate predictors of presidential politics in the country. Since William Jennings Bryan defeated John A. Johnson in 1908, the counterfeit caucus has correctly predicted presidential nominees 18 of 24 times, an accuracy rate of 75 percent. Despite the festive atmosphere, a year's worth of serious research goes into keeping up such a good track record (recently broken in 2008, when Barack Obama was chosen for the Democratic nomination over Hillary Clinton—but that was only the second misfire in choosing the party's nominee in W&L's history). The convention happens early in the actual races, making it the subject of national interest.

Every July, Lexington hosts the **Fourth of July Balloon Rally** at the VMI parade grounds. Activities include piloted balloon flights, tethered balloon rides, live music, fireworks, and children's activities.

---

be arranged through **Twin Rivers Outfitters** (653 Lowe St., Buchanan, 540/261-7334, www.canoevirginia.com) for $15–40 per person. Longer trips are also possible. Based in Natural Bridge Station, the **Wilderness Canoe Company** (631 James River Rd., 540/291-2295, www.wildernesscanoecampground.com) will send you down the James River in a canoe, kayak, or tube ($15–60); prices include shuttle service, maps, and equipment.

SHOPPING

Local artists have formed a cooperative gallery in the Alexander-Withrow House called **Artists in Cahoots** (1 W. Washington St., 540/464-1147), showcasing beautiful crafts from photography and stained glass to hand-painted silks and delicate carved birds. Some artists also work here. **Virginia Born and Bred** (16 W. Washington St., 800/437-2452) stocks Americana like hand-carved nutcrackers and folk art alongside jellies, hams, and wines.

ACCOMMODATIONS

...cing its role as one of the state's most popular getaway towns, the Lexington region is positively rife with guesthouses.

$50-100

Maury Heights Farm (1080 Maury River Rd., 540/463-7458, www.mhfarm.com) offers two guest rooms ($60–90) in a pastoral valley three miles from the visitors center. The building also has a den/office room with Wi-Fi, and rates include a continental breakfast.

Off I-64 exit 55 is a **Super 8 Motel** (1139 N. Lee Hwy., 540/463-7458) with rooms for $70–90.

$100-150

John Roberts, the owner of (**A Bed & Breakfast at Llewellyn Lodge** (603 S. Main St., 540/463-3235 or 800/882-1145, www.llodge.com, $95–190) was born in the Stonewall Jackson house and knows the Lexington area like the back of his hand. He's even written a local hiking guide he's happy to share with guests. His place, a brick Colonial-style building, is the longest-running bed-and-breakfast in town, and rooms include a celebrated full gourmet breakfast cooked by his wife, Ellen. They're happy to help organize fishing and canoeing trips too.

The (**Applewood Inn** (242 Tarn Beck Ln., 540/463-1962 or 800/463-1902, www.applewoodbb.com, $130–155) is an environmentally friendly bed-and-breakfast offering 37 acres of rustic comfort south of town. A California redwood hot tub sits on an enclosed porch that's part of the house's solar envelope construction, where a layer of heated air surrounding the entire building provides warmth well into the night. Guests are welcome to use the pool and kitchen, and the owners offer two-hour llama treks into the hills for guests and day visitors for $18–24 per person. To get there, take Route 11 for 4.5 miles south of town and make a right onto Buffalo Bend Road, following signs for the next 1.2 miles to Tarn Beck Lane.

On U.S. 60, 4.5 miles west of Lexington, is the **Days Inn Lexington** (325 W. Midland Trail, 540/463-2143), with rooms for $82–200.

The **Best Western Inn at Hunt Ridge** (25 Willow Springs Rd., 540/464-1500, $100–120) is a modern place with a Colonial flair. Rates include a continental breakfast. Head north of town on Lee Highway (Rte. 11), cross under I-64, take a quick left on Maury River Road (Rte. 39), and Willow Springs Road will be on your right.

$150-200

The **Magnolia House Inn** (501 S. Main St., 540/463-2567, www.magnoliahouseinn.com) dates to 1868 and boasts high ceilings, spacious rooms, and a cottage garden. Guests are greeted with a cool drink and a warm cookie and can choose from three rooms and two suites ($140–190).

Historic Country Inns of Lexington (11 N. Main St., 877/283-9680, www.lexingtonhistoricinns.com) offers 32 rooms and 12 suites in two beautifully restored historic townhouses downtown—the 1809 **McCampbell Inn** and the 1789 **Alexander-Withrow House**—as well as in the 1850 **Maple Hall Country Inn** seven miles north of town, which comes complete with guest house, pond house, pool, and tennis court. Rooms and suites range in price $110–180, including expanded continental breakfast.

An 1827 manor home has been converted into the **Hampton Inn Lexington** (401 E. Nelson St., 540/463-2223, $144–265), graced by a Palladian porch and many antiques.

Camping

The **Virginia Horse Center** (540/464-2966, www.horsecenter.org) has two campgrounds with water and electric hookups; call for details.

FOOD

Snacks and Cafés

The **Lexington Coffee Shop** (9 W. Washington St., 540/464-6586, breakfast and lunch daily) serves stiff brews and baked goods in a relaxed wood floor–and–burlap atmosphere. The beans are fair trade and freshly roasted each week, and accompanied by free Wi-Fi and occasional live music.

A Joyful Spirit Café (26 S. Main St., 540/463-4191, breakfast Mon.–Sat., lunch daily) is a vegetarian-friendly place serving breakfast, bagels, salads, and grilled sandwiches and wraps for $6–8.

Sweet Things (106 W. Washington St., 540/463-6055, lunch and dinner daily) offers homemade ice cream and frozen yogurt in just about every conceivable permutation, with hand-rolled waffle cones to boot.

Casual

A big green neon sign lights the way to the **Southern Inn** (37 S. Main St., 540/463-3612, lunch and dinner daily), a long high-ceilinged place open since 1932. The Southern-style food is well prepared from scratch, whether it's the roasted portobello mushroom sandwich for lunch ($8–14) or the arugula salad and the sautéed calf's liver and onions for dinner ($12–25).

Southern cooking is on the menu at the Southern Inn, as are fresh salads.

There is a wide selection of wines as well. Try to sit at the bar for a casual, cozy evening buzzing with locals and visitors alike.

The Southern influence continues in a contemporary vein at the **Bistro on Main** (8 N. Main St., 540/464-4888, lunch and dinner Tues.–Sat., brunch Sun.), serving jambalaya, shrimp and grits, and the tasty Bistro burger. Lunch runs $4–9 and dinner $12–24, with fresh seafood specials and vegetarian dishes too.

Upscale

Half a mile from downtown, **Café Michel** (640 N. Lee Hwy., 540/464-4119) offers fine French-inspired fare such as lobster in puff pastry and steak au poivre ($13–23) for dinner Monday–Saturday. In the summer you can sit on the outdoor patio, and the bar room is available for a drink at any time.

Back in town, the jaunty red café on the corner of Washington and Main Streets is the **Red Hen** (11 E. Washington St., 540/464-4401, dinner Tues.–Sat.), a farm-to-table Lexington favorite. In fine weather, grab a seat on the patio. You can catch a glimpse of herbs cultivated for dinner. Plates like seared trout with lentils and bacon run $16–32. Reservations strongly recommended.

Enjoy the tastes of northern Italy at **Tuscany** (24 N. Main St., 540/463-9888), with homemade sauces and desserts complemented by Continental wines. Tuscany is open for lunch and dinner daily (entrées $14–25) and features a piano lounge every evening. The dining room at the **Maple Hall Country Inn** (11 N. Main St., 540/463-2044 or 877/283-9680, www.lexingtonhistoricinns.com) is another excellent option for a fine dinner, with a glass-walled patio and home-baked bread.

INFORMATION

Lexington's well-organized **visitors center** (106 E. Washington St., 540/463-3777 or 877/453-9822, www.lexingtonvirginia.com, 9 A.M.–5 P.M. daily Sept.–May, 8:30 A.M.–6 P.M. daily June–Aug.) features a miniature museum, a short video presentation, and helpful employees.

South of Lexington

NATURAL BRIDGE

Rockbridge County derives its name from this 215-foot-tall limestone span—all that remains of a huge cavern carved out over thousands of years by tiny Cedar Creek. Thomas Jefferson, who once owned Natural Bridge, called it "so beautiful in archeology, so elevated, so light, and springing as it were up to Heaven, [that] the rapture of the spectator is really indescribable."

Natural Bridge is spectacular, to be sure—it's one of Virginia's most impressive natural sights. Almost as fascinating, though, is what has evolved around it. Interstate billboards are stacked like dominoes for hundreds of miles in every direction, and even ticket sellers can't keep a straight face describing the nightly *Drama of Creation* colored-light show, complete with music and solemn narration on the origins of the universe. If you run out of money, there's an ATM; if you find religion, there's a Baptist church. In the end, the whole package, which has little to do with the bridge, gives a new shade of meaning to the slogan "the Wonder of It All."

History

According to native legend, the "Bridge of God" materialized to help a band of Monocan Indians fleeing from raiding Shawnee and Powhatans. In 1749, British Lord Fairfax hired Col. Peter Jefferson—who, six years earlier, had fathered a son destined to become president—to survey the land around today's Route 11. One young assistant carved his initials on the stone wall; the faint "GW" is still visible, making George Washington the only president to have officially defaced a Virginia landmark. In 1773, Thomas Jefferson gained title to the bridge and 157 surrounding acres from King George III for 20 shillings. Near the base he built a log cabin and installed a "sentiment" book in which prominent visitors could record their impressions. During the Revolutionary War, soldiers made bullets by pouring molten lead from the bridge into the creek below and mined saltpeter from nearby caves for gunpowder.

The Bridge

All visits to the bridge (800/533-1410, www.naturalbridgeva.com, 8 A.M.–dusk daily) start at the main ticket building, which encloses a gargantuan gift shop, an indoor pool, a miniature golf course, an ATM, and a post office. Brochures in French, German, Spanish, Russian, Chinese, and Japanese describe what you're going to see, as soon as you've decided which ticket package to buy. Options include the bridge and the wax and toy museums only ($18 adults, $10 children 5–12), or the bridge, museums, and caverns ($26/$14). (The bridge and toy museum are open year-round, but the other attractions are closed in the off-season.) You can drive over the bridge for free—Route 11 heading east toward the Blue Ridge Parkway

Natural Bridge

crosses right over it—but you can't see anything from above.

Walk downhill or take a shuttle bus to the beginning of the trail, where the **Summer House Cafe** offers light fare in an open patio alongside the creek. Children's voices echo up the deep, wooded gorge, where you'll get your first glimpse of the sheer size of the thing. At 50–150 feet wide and 90 feet long, it's massive, but surprisingly graceful for 36,000 tons of stone. The trail continues along the creek, a pleasant walk when it's not too crowded. Past an open space where Easter sunrise services have been held since 1947 are an old saltpeter mine, picnic areas, and the Lace Waterfalls.

Other Sights

George Washington, Daniel Boone, and Robert E. Lee share quarters with some 175 others in the **Natural Bridge Wax Museum** (10 A.M.–5 P.M. daily). Narrated historic scenes include the Garden of Eden and a theatrical presentation of Leonardo da Vinci's *Last Supper*. An explanation of the making of wax figures is part of the tour.

It's said that the ghost of a woman haunts the **Natural Bridge Caverns** (10 A.M.–5 P.M. daily Mar.–Nov.), the deepest cave on the East Coast. Guided tours to spots including the Wishing Well Room, Colossal Dome Room, and Mirror Lake leave every half hour.

The **Toy Museum** (10 A.M.–5 P.M. daily) is billed as the largest collection of childhood memorabilia on display in the world. More than 45,000 toys, games, and dolls range from Revolutionary War–era dolls to Star Wars figures.

Natural Bridge Zoo (540/291-2420, www.naturalbridgezoo.com, 10 A.M.–5 P.M. daily Mar.–Nov., longer hours in early summer and on weekends, $12 adults, $8 children), on Route 11 south, harbors the usual—giraffes, camels, bears, and monkeys—along with rare and endangered species such as a white tiger born in 1997. It also boasts the largest petting zoo in the state. If you haven't had your critter fix by now, stop by the **Virginia Safari Park** (540/291-3205, www.virginiasafaripark.com, 9 A.M.–5 P.M. daily Mar.–May and Sept.–Nov., until 6 P.M. Apr.–Oct., $14 adults, $10 children 3–12), a 180-acre drive-through zoo. A three-mile road takes you past bison, zebra, antelope, and ostriches roaming free (more or less), and there's also a petting zoo, an aviary, and a primate house. Kids love the giraffe feeding station. Wagon rides ($4 pp) run at 1 and 3 P.M. on weekends.

A tour of **Professor Cline's Haunted Monster Museum and Dark Maze** (4942 S. Lee Hwy., 540/464-2253, 11 A.M.–7 P.M. daily June–Aug., noon–5 P.M. weekends in spring and fall, closed in winter, $8 adults, $5 children) begins with your greeter, in top hat and tails, leading you into the former Stonewall Inn and locking the only door behind you. You have no choice but to proceed onward, past moving bookcases, the professor's secret lab, lunging monsters, and rattling séance tables. (The scare factor can be toned down for small children.)

Accommodations and Food

Next to the ticket building, the **Natural Bridge Hotel** (800/533-1410) has rooms in the hotel year-round for $70–140 and four- to six-room cottages across the road starting at $82 (mid-Mar.–Oct.). There's also an Olympic-sized pool and a restaurant serving all meals daily, with outdoor dining on the veranda and popular weekend buffets. Various packages include lodging, meals, and admission to the attractions.

Yogi Bear's Jellystone Park Camp-Resort at Natural Bridge (540/291-2727 or 800/258-9532, www.campnbr.com) has full-hookup sites for $44–54, tent spots for $40, and cabins for $90–160 per night. It rents boats, canoes, and tubes to enjoy the nearby James River and charges a small fee for fishing in its stocked pond. To get there, take Route 130 east from I-81 exit 175 for 4.5 miles, take a right onto Route 759, then your first left onto Route 782. Sites at the **Natural Bridge KOA** (540/291-2770, www.naturalbridgekoa.com) are $25–50. It's just off I-81 exit 180 on Route 11.

HUMPBACK COVERED BRIDGE

Virginia's oldest covered bridge spans Dunlap Creek, three miles west of Covington on U.S. 60. Built in 1835, Humpback Covered Bridge was restored for foot traffic in 1953, and the surrounding land was set aside as a park and picnic area. Ropes dangle underneath for (illicit) swings into the water, and the inside of the bridge, sadly, is defaced by graffiti. It's one of only eight covered bridges in Virginia, three of which are on private property.

Near Natural Bridge

Since no natural wonder is complete without a replica megalithic observatory, don't miss **Foamhenge**, a full-sized model sculpted in foam blocks, one mile north of the bridge (free). Six miles east of Natural Bridge on Route 130 is the tiny town of **Glasgow**, "the Town That Time Forgot," where a dozen full-size dinosaur replicas have invaded buildings and backyards.

A short drive up into the Jefferson National Forest brings you to the **Cave Mountain Lake Recreation Area** (540/291-2188, www.fs.fed.us/r8/gwj/gp), centered on a cold, clear seven-acre lake formed in the 1930s by a dam built by the Civilian Conservation Corps. It's popular for swimming and fishing, with showers and a sandy beach area, and there's a log picnic shelter available. Campsites are $15–30 each (open May–Oct.). Hikers can choose from the half-mile Panther Knob Natural Trail or the four-mile Wildcat Mountain Trail loop. Head further afield into the nearby James River Face Wilderness, the state's first designated wilderness. It's bisected by the Appalachian Trail and miles of other hiking paths, including the route up the Devil's Marbleyard.

To get to Cave Mountain Lake, take Route 130 east from I-81 exit 175 or 180 for 3.2 miles, turn south onto Route 795 for another 3.2 miles, and turn right onto Route 781 for 1.6 miles to the recreation area's paved entrance road.

BLUE RIDGE PARKWAY

Like a vine connecting two ripe grapes, this scenic highway unites the Shenandoah and Great Smoky Mountains National Parks in one long, lovely stretch of Appalachia. It was begun during

Foamhenge, a full-sized replica of Stonehenge, near Natural Bridge

the Great Depression as a federal public-works project. Designers took liberties with the philosophy of the shortest distance between two points, choosing instead to follow the wandering ridgeline wherever it chose to go. Of the parkway's 469 miles, 217 are in Virginia, and the first 114, between Waynesboro and Roanoke along the crest of the Blue Ridge Mountains, are widely thought to be the most impressive. Miles of tranquil farm scenes are punctuated by crumbling graveyards and "gaps," which open to grand panoramas in either direction. The Appalachian Trail follows the parkway from the northern end at Rockfish Gap south to Roanoke, where it veers off to the west. In 2010, the Blue Ridge Parkway celebrated its 75th anniversary.

Access

The parkway is open year-round, although few facilities outside Peaks of Otter are open beyond May–October, and parts of the road may be closed due to inclement weather. In foggy conditions, blinking lights lining the road are sometimes your only guiderail, so be careful. Entry is free. Between I-64 at Waynesboro and U.S. 460 at Roanoke, drivers can reach the road via U.S. 60 near Buena Vista, Routes 30 and 501 east of Natural Bridge, and Route 43 between Bedford and Buchanan.

Flora and Fauna

Vegetation along the parkway is more southern (drier) than in Shenandoah National Park. Forests of white pine, hemlock, and hawthorn burst into color during an extended fall season, thanks to the wide range of altitudes along the entire road (649–6,047 ft.). In the autumn spectrum, reds are probably maples or dogwoods, yellows hickory, and orange sassafras. Spruce, fir, and pine provide a green backdrop. Spectacular flame azalea bloom throughout the park in May and June, followed by purple Catawba rhododendron near Peaks of Otter in June. Many of the larger animals come out at dusk and are gone by dawn, leaving daytime to the groundhogs, squirrels, and chipmunks. White-tailed deer, bobcats, raccoons, and black bears all make occasional appearances.

Camping

Of the four campgrounds along the Virginia section of the Blue Ridge Parkway, two are north of Roanoke: **Otter Creek** (434/299-5941, Apr.–Oct., $16), on the James River at the parkway's lowest elevation, and **Peaks of Otter** (540/586-4357, mid-May–Oct., $16), at milepost 86 near the Peaks of Otter Lodge. Campsites in Virginia are first-come, first-served, and limited to a 21-day maximum stay. Some are accessible to visitors with disabilities. Trailers up to 30 feet are permitted, and all campgrounds have dump stations (but no water or electrical hookups). Pets must be kept on leashes. Off the parkway, backcountry camping is permitted in the George Washington National Forest.

Rockfish Gap to Sherando Lake

All locations along the parkway are measured in mileposts (mp), from milepost 0 at the southern end of Shenandoah National Park at Rockfish Gap to milepost 218 at the North Carolina border. The speed limit along the entire parkway is 45 mph, but traffic can crawl during high season.

At the **Humpback Rocks Visitor Center** (mp 5.8), a self-guided trail leads through a reconstructed 19th-century farmstead, with exhibits on life in the rural Blue Ridge. Across the road, a steep 0.75-mile trail climbs to the jagged top of Humpback Rocks (3,080 ft.) for a 360-degree view of the mountains. Watching the sun rise from the top of Humpback with a steaming Thermos of coffee is one of the best vistas in the whole state. Past **Devil's Knob** (3,851 ft.) is a turn-off to Route 664 east toward Wintergreen Ski Resort.

Head west on Route 664 to reach the **Sherando Lake Recreation Area,** centered on a pair of lakes created in the early 1900s by the Civilian Conservation Corps for recreation and flood control. The 25-acre lower lake is open to swimming and boating, with a sandy swimming beach, while the seven-acre lake above it is known for trout, bass, and bluegill fishing. There are 65 campsites arranged around three loops near the water.

Mountain biking enthusiasts know Sherando as the home of one of the burliest trails in this part of the state. Head up the steep, rocky Blue Loop trail past the lake toward the park entrance—you'll end up carrying your bike, trust me—to the yellow-blazed Torrey Ridge Trail 1,000 feet above. Go down the ridgeline, carrying your bike yet again through a nasty rock garden, then head down the blue-blazed Slacks Trail to the orange-blazed White Rock Trail back to the lake. The whole thing is an 11-mile loop, and all the carrying makes the ride down that much sweeter.

Sherando Lake to Otter Creek

Below the **Twenty Minute Cliff Overlook,** the Tye River spills east to eventually join the James. At **Tye River Gap** (2,969 ft.), take narrow, winding Route 56 east to the trailhead for **Crabtree Falls Trail,** leading to the highest waterfall east of the Mississippi. Five large waterfalls and many smaller ones tumble over 1,200 feet all told. It's best in the spring, when the water levels are high. An easy trail with steps and railings leads along the water, which can be filled with splashing families in the summer. There's a good rock for picnicking at the top. You can also access the three-mile trail from above, at a parking lot on Route 826 (4WD only) at Crabtree Meadows, where it's possible to make a primitive camp.

This is also a good spot to access two of the state's newest and choicest wilderness areas. The 5,742-acre **Priest Wilderness** encloses eight peaks higher than 4,000 feet, including the Priest (4,063 ft.), the Friar, and the Cardinal. The 4,748-acre **Three Ridges Wilderness** is probably one of the most rugged and wild sections of Virginia's Blue Ridge. Both were set aside in 2000 and are connected to the parkway by the Appalachian Trail.

Yankee Horse (mp 34.4) is named for an unfortunate Union mount that had to be shot after it fell from exhaustion. Here an overlook trail leads along a remnant of an old logging railway from the 1920s to 30-foot Wigwam Falls in a shady grove.

Otter Creek to Roanoke

The **Otter Creek Campground** (mp 60.8) has 69 sites ($16), a coffee shop, and a service station. The creek rolls down the hillside toward the James River, lined by blooming mountain laurel in May and June.

The parkway hits its lowest point (649 ft.) where it crosses the James River. Here you'll find a visitors center at the **James River Overlook** (mp 63.6). A self-guiding trail leads over a footbridge and along the river bluff to restored locks along the Kanawha canal.

After climbing to its highest point in Virginia (3,950 ft.), the parkway winds into the **Peaks of Otter** (mp 86), with a visitors center, 151 campsites, and the **Peaks of Otter Lodge** (540/586-1081 or 800/542-5927, www.peaksofotter.com), the only place on the parkway guaranteed to be open year-round. Sixty rooms overlooking Abbott Lake each have two double beds but no TVs or phones, with prices around $115–130 (as low as $85 in off-season). The view from the dining room is justly famous, and the hotel has two restaurants, a lounge, and a gift shop. Trails near the campground lead to the restored 1930s Johnson Farm. Thought to be the highest point in the state by Thomas Jefferson, Sharp Top (3,875 ft.) can be reached by foot and sweat via a steep 1.5-mile trail, or on a tour bus from the hotel that drops you off near the peak.

From here it's another 34 miles to the campground at Roanoke Mountain.

Information

The Blue Ridge Parkway is administered by the National Park Service in Asheville, North Carolina (828/298-0398 or 828/271-4779, www.nps.gov/blri). Each visitors center sells excellent books detailing hikes, history, and wildlife along the road. **Friends of the Blue Ridge Parkway** (800/228-7275, www.blueridgefriends.org) is a nonprofit volunteer organization dedicated to preserving and protecting the parkway. For more information, check out the Blue Ridge Parkway Association's online travel guide (www.blueridgeparkway.org).

www.moon.com

DESTINATIONS | ACTIVITIES | BLOGS | MAPS | BOOKS

MOON.COM is ready to help plan your next trip! Filled with fresh trip ideas and strategies, author interviews, informative travel blogs, a detailed map library, and descriptions of all the Moon guidebooks, Moon.com is all you need to get out and explore the world—or even places in your own backyard. While at Moon.com, sign up for our monthly e-newsletter for updates on new releases, travel tips, and expert advice from our on-the-go Moon authors. As always, when you travel with Moon, expect an experience that is uncommon and truly unique.

MOON IS ON FACEBOOK—BECOME A FAN!
JOIN THE MOON PHOTO GROUP ON FLICKR

MAP SYMBOLS

Expressway	ⓒ Highlight	✈ Airport	Ⓜ Metro
Primary Road	○ City/Town	✕ Airfield	Ⓟ Parking Area
Secondary Road	⊚ State Capital	▲ Mountain	Golf Course
Unpaved Road	⊛ National Capital	✦ Unique Natural Feature	Church
Trail	★ Point of Interest	Waterfall	Gas Station
Ferry	• Accommodation	▲ Park	Glacier
Railroad	▼ Restaurant/Bar	Trailhead	Mangrove
Pedestrian Walkway	■ Other Location	Skiing Area	Reef
Stairs	▲ Campground	Battlefield	Swamp

CONVERSION TABLES

°C = (°F − 32) / 1.8
°F = (°C × 1.8) + 32
1 inch = 2.54 centimeters (cm)
1 foot = 0.304 meters (m)
1 yard = 0.914 meters
1 mile = 1.6093 kilometers (km)
1 km = 0.6214 miles
1 fathom = 1.8288 m
1 chain = 20.1168 m
1 furlong = 201.168 m
1 acre = 0.4047 hectares
1 sq km = 100 hectares
1 sq mile = 2.59 square km
1 ounce = 28.35 grams
1 pound = 0.4536 kilograms
1 short ton = 0.90718 metric ton
1 short ton = 2,000 pounds
1 long ton = 1.016 metric tons
1 long ton = 2,240 pounds
1 metric ton = 1,000 kilograms
1 quart = 0.94635 liters
1 US gallon = 3.7854 liters
1 Imperial gallon = 4.5459 liters
1 nautical mile = 1.852 km

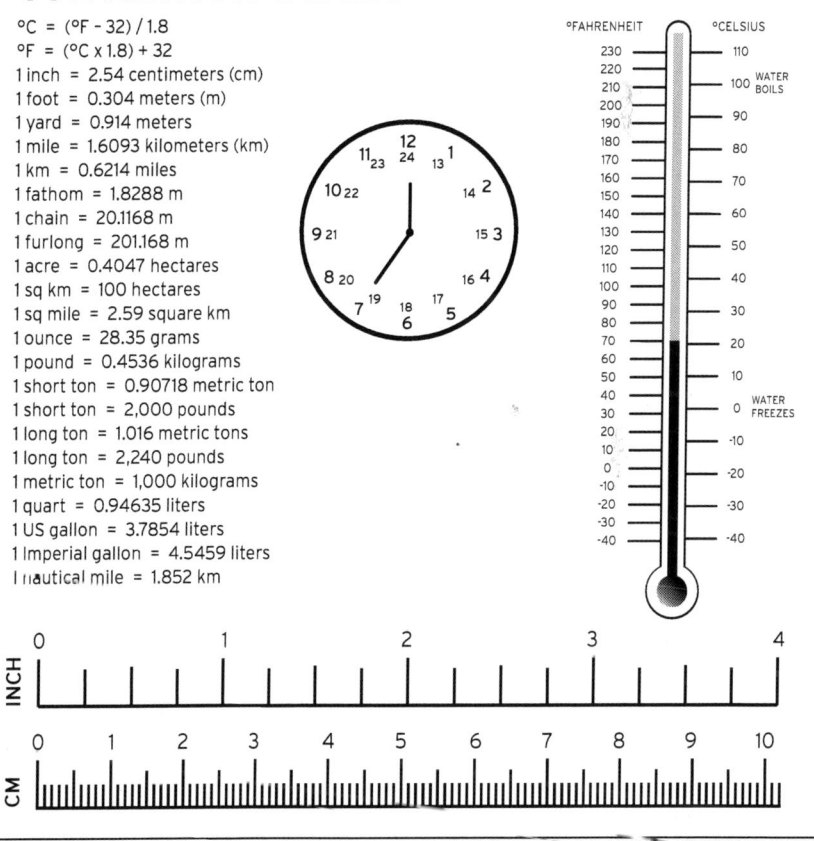

MOON SPOTLIGHT
VIRGINIA'S SHENANDOAH
Avalon Travel
a member of the Perseus Books Group
1700 Fourth Street
Berkeley, CA 94710, USA
www.moon.com

Editor and Series Manager: Kathryn Ettinger
Copy Editor: Amy Scott
Graphics Coordinator: Elizabeth Jang
Production Coordinator: Elizabeth Jang
Cover Designer: Kathryn Osgood
Map Editor: Albert Angulo
Cartographers: Kat Bennett, Allison Rawley

ISBN: 978-1-59880-670-0

Text © 2010 by Katie Githens and Avalon Travel.
Maps © 2010 by Avalon Travel.
All rights reserved.

Some photos and illustrations are used by permission and are the property of the original copyright owners.

Front cover photo: A view of peaks above rolling fog along Skyline Drive in Shenandoah National Park © Craig Doros / Dreamstime.com
Title page photo: Humpback Covered Bridge near Covington © John P. Mueller

Printed in the United States

Moon Spotlight and the Moon logo are the property of Avalon Travel. All other marks and logos depicted are the property of the original owners. All rights reserved. No part of this book may be translated or reproduced in any form, except brief extracts by a reviewer for the purpose of a review, without written permission of the copyright owner.

All recommendations, including those for sights, activities, hotels, restaurants, and shops, are based on each author's individual judgment. We do not accept payment for inclusion in our travel guides, and our authors don't accept free goods or services in exchange for positive coverage.

Although every effort was made to ensure that the information was correct at the time of going to press, the author and publisher do not assume and hereby disclaim any liability to any party for any loss or damage caused by errors, omissions, or any potential travel disruption due to labor or financial difficulty, whether such errors or omissions result from negligence, accident, or any other cause.

ABOUT THE AUTHOR

© MORGANA WINGARD

Katie Githens

Travel writer Katie Githens already had her nose to the ground, so to speak, exploring the best of Virginia when she started her research for *Moon Spotlight Virginia's Shenandoah*. Her first book, *The Dog Lover's Companion to Washington DC* (which includes northern Virginia in its coverage), was still hot off the presses when she set off to explore the Shenandoah.

Katie learned a few things during her travels: namely, that bluegrass is soul music; that she would have aced American history if she grew up here; and that knowing how to drive on winding country roads in winter is a very, very useful skill to have.

While doing the footwork for *Moon Spotlight Virginia's Shenandoah*, Katie kept one eye peeled for outdoor adventure. She loves nothing more than a good, long trail run, except maybe a farmers market to stop at for breakfast when she's done.

Before moving to Arlington County in 2005, Katie wrapped up a journalism degree from beachfront Pepperdine University and honed her writing skills at *The Aspen Times* and *Los Angeles Sports & Fitness* magazine. When she's not researching a project that puts her behind the wheel or holding a leash, Katie is behind a desk as a writer and editor in support of the U.S. Environmental Protection Agency. She lives in Arlington with her husband, Mike Githens, and her dog and frequent travel companion, Denali.